T

DATE DUE			

THE
ANTHROPOLOGY OF
DANCE

Anya Peterson Royce

INDIANA UNIVERSITY PRESS
BLOOMINGTON AND LONDON

FIRST MIDLAND BOOK EDITION 1980

Copyright © 1977 by Anya Peterson Royce

Manufactured in the United States of America

Library of Congress Cataloging in Publication Data
Royce, Anya Peterson.
The anthropology of dance.
Bibliography: p.
Includes index.
1. Dance and society.   I. Title.
GV1588.6.R7 1977   793.3'01   77-74428
ISBN 0-253-30752-X   2 3 4 5 81 80
ISBN 0-253-20235-3 pbk.

To Ron

Contents

ILLUSTRATIONS

Acknowledgments

field research which has been funded by a variety of institutions. My research with the two powwow groups in the San Francisco Bay Area occurred while I was a graduate student at the University of California at Berkeley supported by a National Institute of Health training grant, which also funded my research in Juchitán with the Isthmus Zapotec in 1971-72. Further research among the Zapotec in the summer of 1974 was financed by a grant-in-aid of research from the Latin American Studies program of Indiana University.

Many ideas were generated by an international conference, "New Directions in the Anthropology of Dance," held here at Indiana University in the spring of 1972. Institutions and programs that supported that conference were the Committee on International Conferences and Seminars of Indiana University, the African Studies, Latin American Studies, and Russian and East European Studies programs of Indiana University, the Department of Anthropology of Indiana University, and the International Research and Exchanges Board. In particular, I would like to thank Alan Merriam and George M. Wilson for their active encouragement of that conference.

A number of people deserve my gratitude for their substantial contributions to the actual putting together of the manuscript. Kathleen Figgen did much of the bibliographic search and the preliminary typing. Rita Brown and Sally Detzler also aided in the initial typing. Ellen Freudenthal did an excellent job of searching out illustrative material. Gloria Young did the final typing of the manuscript. As valuable as her services in that regard were her critical comments on the manuscript. All of that and her unfailing good humor and patience I greatly appreciate.

At the beginning I said that this book was the direct result of my husband's influence. Though I might eventually have written it without his provocation, that it has been written now is entirely his doing. We have touched upon most of the material in the book over the past ten years, discussing it more intensively while the book was actually in the writing. Many of the ideas are his; certainly much of the refinement of ideas results from his influence. His tangible contributions include the art work for figures 4 and 6 and the index for the book. For all this, I thank him.

A.P.R.

Bloomington, Indiana
April, 1976

THE ANTHROPOLOGY OF DANCE

PART ONE

The Anthropology of Dance

❧ 1 ❧

THE DANCE

DANCE HAS BEEN called the oldest of the arts. It is perhaps equally true that it is older than the arts. The human body making patterns in time and space is what makes the dance unique among the arts and perhaps explains its antiquity and universality.

There are two problems for those who would draw boundaries around the phenomenon of dance. First is the question of whether dance is exclusively a human activity or whether it can be attributed to nonhumans as well; and second is the problem of distinguishing dance from other closely related activities. Both problems arise from the fact that dance results from the body making patterns in time and space.

The reliance of dance on a very basic instrument, the human body, has led people to draw parallels between the dancing of human and nonhuman primates and to speak of the dancing of birds, bees, and sticklebacks. Curt Sachs, for example, cites two wonderful examples of birds dancing:

> The birds . . . were long-legged creatures, tall almost as storks, and white and grey of feather; and the dance took place in the center of a broad, dry swamp. . . . There were some hundreds of them, and their dance was in the manner of a quadrille, but in

3

the matter of rhythm and grace excelling any quadrille that ever was. In groups of a score or more they advanced and retreated, lifting high their long legs and standing on their toes, now and then bowing gracefully to one another, now and then one pair encircling with prancing daintiness a group whose heads moved upwards and downwards and sideways in time to the stepping of the pair. At times they formed into one great prancing mass, with their long necks thrust upward; and the wide swaying of their backs was like unto the swaying of the sea. Then, suddenly, as in response to an imperative command, they would sway apart, some of them to rise in low, encircling flight, and some to stand as in little gossiping groups; and presently they would form in pairs or sets of pairs, and the prancing and the bowing, and advancing and retreating would begin all over again (Maclaren 1926, *in* Sachs 1937:9,10).

The second example, which comes from British Guiana, is even more interesting since it describes what is essentially a performer-spectator situation:

a group of some twenty mountain chickens of brilliant orange-yellow color, gathered together in a kind of dance characteristic of these beautiful birds. In the center one of the cocks executed the dance-like movements, as he hopped about the open place with wings extended and tail outspread. On the branches of the bushes round about, the others sat and expressed their admiration of the dancer with the strangest sounds. As soon as one cock was exhausted, he joined the spectators . . . and another took his place (Apun 1871, *in* Sachs 1937:9).

Sachs resolves what he feels is a potential problem, whether in fact we can speak of what animals do as dance, by making the distinction between innate and acquired characteristics. The problem becomes knotty once more, however, when one considers the dancing of chimpanzees, where there is an uncomfortable fuzziness about the innate-acquired distinction.

The absence of an instrument separable from man, or rather the fact that in dance the creator and the means of

4

expression (instrument) are one and the same, has also given rise to endless yet understandable confusion between dance and other forms of rhythmical movement. In other words, when is a parade a dance?

Basic to all definitions of the dance is the concept of rhythmic or patterned movement. Obviously this is not sufficient to distinguish dance from many other kinds of rhythmic activities: swimming, working, playing tennis, hollowing out a canoe, to name a few. Although one has to be wary of definitions that are so narrow as to exclude those classes of phenomena which might legitimately be included, one must be able to define one's particular phenomenon so as to remove it from a category too general.

Returning once more to existing definitions of the dance, we find another concept which most writers share: dance is rhythmic movement done for some purpose transcending utility. Adding this concept at once excludes a great many activities that we had to include given only the idea of patterned movement. It may conceivably exclude some activities that might legitimately be dance. On the whole, however, it is the most positive or inclusive of those distinguishing features that we might incorporate in our definitions.

Into the confusion of human versus nonhuman and dance versus nondance comes an additional distinction: that between dance which is essentially an aesthetic activity and dance which serves some other function as well. The history of dance literature reflects this dichotomy, with those who write about "art" dance rigidly separating themselves from those who write about "folk" dance. The distinction actually serves little purpose, and it disappears altogether when one considers dance as an aspect of human behavior.

The ability to describe what one is talking about in such a way as to distinguish it from other phenomena is a matter of crucial importance to scientists, humanists, and people in general. It is of some interest to note, for example, that what we may conceive of as a tree is not a tree to everyone else but, in

5

some parts of the United States, may be referred to as a bush. Stranger still, in some parts of the world this tree-bush may metamorphose into a kind of grass. Definitions, or "categories," make much of life simpler by enabling us to sort out the wealth of stimuli that constantly assault our senses. The process of definition is not without pitfalls and I will discuss some of them at a later point.

It is generally recognized that human beings continually engage in the process of categorization, that is, we go through life putting things into pigeonholes. Most of the time this is an unconscious act. We have grown up learning to recognize features or sets of features by which we may identify all these items in our personal universe. For example, we learn that the set of features composed of four legs, fur, a long tail, small size, pointed ears, whiskers, harelip, and a meow is complete enough and at the same time exclusive enough to let us identify anything with all those features as a cat. Recognition is important because it allows us to respond with the appropriate behavior. Confronted with something that we can put into the category "cat," we know how to react. Change one feature, say that of size, so that instead of a fourteen-pound cat we have a four-hundred-pound cat, and we must change our categories and also our behavior. For the most part, however, our pigeonholing devices serve us well and we would undoubtedly choose the appropriate behavior to fit the "cat" situation without spending much time in reflection and analysis of features.

The preceding is a fairly straightforward example. Let us turn to one that is more complicated and therefore involves more conscious reflection. The custom of shaking hands used to involve many fewer recognitions in the past than it does now. On meeting someone you had only to identify their sex and their status with regard to your own. On the basis of these two fairly simple features you knew whether or not to shake their hand. The proper behavior varied from region to region but by and large men shook the hands of other men who were of approximately the same status; women did not shake hands with men although they did occasionally with other women. Today this same greeting can cause a person indecision. The entrance of women into professions, the greater mobility for both sexes, the increased interaction between people of varied ethnic and social backgrounds—all of these factors have served to complicate what was initially a straightforward greeting ritual. Now upon meeting someone you must define them in terms of sex, relative social status, professional status, and ethnic background. Even then, assuming that you have made the proper identifications, the fact that you may be in a different part of the United States may invalidate all of your assumptions and you will find yourself committing social faux pas in spite of all your best intentions.

What we may conclude from this discussion is that categorization is a necessary adjunct to man's life as a social animal, that most of the time it is an almost automatic process and one in which we operate fairly smoothly, and finally that difficulties arise when we move from the middle ground of categories to the borders. It has always been the boundaries, the fuzzy fringes, the dividing lines between phenomena that have created problems of definition and categorization. And if you look at the development of any field of inquiry, you will find scholars drawn inexorably to those fringes, mesmerized like snakes by dancing mongooses. This is not totally without merit for it gives us the whetstone on which to sharpen our intellectual tools. It is also a source of pride in disciplinary coherence because by carefully defining what it is we are or do, we separate ourselves from all those others occupying adjacent pigeonholes. Then, too, we must be able to define the subject matter of our inquiry in order to say anything significant about it or in order to be able to draw comparisons.

Our initial dilemma about the proper degree of exclusivity of definitions can be solved easily. We must have an adequate working definition of dance about which there is a measure of agreement. It should define the field rather more inclusively than exclusively. In other words, it should be the minimal definition necessary to allow us to agree on phenomena that occur in the middle of the category "dance." Such definitions already exist (see, for example, Kurath, 1960; Hanna, 1965, 1973; Kealiinohomoku, 1965, rev. 1970). A streamlined definition, but one which still includes the two concepts basic to almost all definitions of dance, would be one which defines dance as "patterned movement performed as an end in itself."

There is an additional factor crucial to any discussion of definitions in general, and definitions of dance in particular. The only reason for the existence of definitions is to allow us to talk about something and have others understand what it is. But there are two levels of understanding: one between analysts and another that has significance for natives. As scholars of the dance, we may create more and more sophisticated definitions of the dance, but they are only useful as analytic devices in that they may or may not correspond to definitions of dance that are meaningful to those engaged in the particular dance form. If they do happen to correspond to something in the real world, they are rarely meaningful to more than a few societies and they are certainly never universal. It would be silly to argue in favor of going out to look at dance "uncontaminated" by any definition at all. It is useful to have some idea of the general features by which we can recognize something as dance. But to take a very narrow definition of dance and force the phenomena into it is to distort the situation and defeat the purpose of the anthropological approach to dance.

Waterman has discussed the problem of needing an analyst's definition and at the same time remaining true to the culture's definitions.

If we stick to aboriginal terminology—and this would undoubtedly result in portraying aboriginal thought about the dance with maximal fidelity—how can we discuss meaningfully an entire category of human behavior that finds no recognition in this terminology? As a result of wrestling with this and allied conceptual problems, anthropologists have come to rely largely on minimal definitions for their own ordering and reporting of data, while carefully preserving and defining the native terms that come closest to having equivalents in our own vocabulary (1962:47).

What we, as anthropologists, must consider are people's perceptions and explanations of the features that make up their particular universe. This, at least, is the starting point from which all further analysis, comparison, and generalization proceeds. Therefore, with dance, as with other aspects of human behavior, we look for the culturally relevant definition.

Let us take some examples of culturally relevant definitions of dance which may not correspond to definitions of dance derived from a basically Western point of view. In speaking of the Australian aborigines of northeastern Arnhem Land, Waterman tells us that the word which comes closest to our word "dance" is *bongol* but that this includes music as well as dance. At the same time, *bongol* may be used in a narower sense than we would find comfortable where it excludes the patterned steps and movements of some of the sacred ceremonies and of certain activities of children's age groups.

The inclusion of music, dance, games, instruments, festivals, and so on within one word is not at all uncommon. In pre-Columbian Mexico, for example, music and dance were linked quite closely, both in thought and in practice, and this is still true of indigenous Mexico today. In Mixtec, the word *yaa* means "dance, game, and music." Further, the same adjectives are often applied to both music and dance. *Kaa/saa* means "high, loud, and strong" when applied to voices; it also means "to sound a high-pitched, loud, or metallic wind instrument," and "to jump" when applied to the dance (Stanford 1966:103). Isthmus Zapotec makes no distinction between "festival" and "music," both being translated as *saa*.

It is not only the non-Western languages and cultures that include several phenomena under one term. Take, for example, the phrase "going to a dance" as it is used in the U.S. The term "dance" here encompasses many things besides the actual physical activity. It includes the music, the interaction with other participants, the refreshments, indeed, the entire ambience of the event. In fact, dancing may be the least important of the activities found at a dance.

The opposite kind of use also occurs, where "dance" is used in a more exclusive sense than we might wish to define it. Generally this takes the form of more than one term for the activities we might classify simply as "dance." Frequently the several terms describe the different contexts of the dance. Spanish, for example, has two words for dance, *danza* and *baile,* which refer to dance as a ritual activity (*danza*) and secular dance (*baile*). Italian makes the same distinction with *danza* and *ballo.* In the classical dance traditions of India, a distinction is made between *nrtta,* "pure dance," and *nrtya,* "pantomimic dance." The danger for the anthropologist looking at dance in unfamiliar cultures lies in the possibility of remaining unaware of the total range of dance activity. For example, should one formulate all questions regarding dance using the term *ballo,* he or she would probably only learn about popular dance. These problems and some solutions will be discussed in the next two chapters.

We have seen thus far that there are at least two kinds of definitions of dance possible, those constructed by dance scholars and those meaningful to specific cultures. I have also indicated the problems in trying to reconcile the two kinds of definitions. Part of our difficulty in coming to terms with definitions is our tendency to separate the form of dance from its context, and whether consciously or not, to use form as the primary basis for definitions. We can resolve much of this difficulty by thinking in terms of *dance events* (see Kealiinohomoku, 1973) rather than of dances and dancing. To illustrate the advantages of taking whole events as the unit of analysis rather than individual dances, I will discuss weddings and the dances associated with them among the Isthmus Zapotec of Mexico.

The Zapotec, which number around 250,000, are located

10

almost exclusively in the state of Oaxaca. The Isthmus Zapotec
live in the southern portion of Oaxaca along the Pacific coast
portion of the Isthmus of Tehuantepec. Although they are
primarily town and small city dwellers in a culturally heterogeneous area, they actively maintain an identity as Zapotec.
One of the features of Zapotec identity is the dance form
known as the *son* and one of the occasions that calls forth the
dancing of *sones* is the wedding. By observing enough dance
behavior at weddings, you can begin to say what is the minimal
amount of dance essential, what is usual, and what are the
outside limits. As a minimum, the sponsor of the young couple
hires one band which can play both *sones* and *piezas* (these terms
refer to both the music and the dance and the lyrics, if any; a
son is a traditional dance form while a *pieza* is any Western social
dance). *Sones* and *piezas* are played and danced alternately
throughout the festivities. At a certain point during the afternoon the bride and groom must begin the *mediu xhiga,* a special
son performed only at weddings. Without these kinds of dances,
the *sones,* the *piezas,* and the *mediu xhiga,* the event is not considered a proper wedding. There are additional dances which
may be done but which do not figure in the minimal definition
of wedding. These include "La Cola" and "La Escoba" (literally,
"The Tail" and "The Broom"), both of which are noncouple
dances, unlike *sones* and *piezas.* In certain weddings the political
and social interests of the various parties may encourage a
demonstration of Zapotec ethnic identity. In such circumstances the proportion of *sones* danced increases greatly in relation to the number of *piezas.* Weddings of wealthy persons usually involve a greater number of both kinds of dances, as well as
of "La Cola" and "La Escoba." Only the performance of the
mediu xhiga remains invariable: it is performed once, and only
once, at every wedding. The selection and sequence of dances
at a Zapotec wedding make sense within the total context of
Zapotec culture, and any changes in the selection or sequence
give you information you would not have if you viewed each
dance as an isolated occurrence.

One might argue that what I have described is not a *dance*

event but is rather a *wedding* event. First, since one cannot have a wedding without dance, the dance event and the wedding event are in a certain sense the same thing. Second, there are very few dance events where dance is the only feature. Even where dance is performed in a theatrical setting, which is probably the closest thing to a pure dance event, there is the crucial factor of interaction between dancers and nondancers. One simply has to observe those occasions where dance is performed and observe them in their entirety.

The real difficulty lies not in distinguishing the dance event *per se,* but rather in drawing boundaries around "events" or "situations." Again, the analyst's divisions may be arbitrary and so once again we must discover the boundaries that are culturally meaningful. To the analyst a Zapotec wedding may be four days of feasting, dancing, processions, and religious and civil ceremonies. To a Zapotec, however, a wedding may have been a year in the making. If the wedding is by petition rather than by elopement, then it might "begin" with the asking for the bride by the groom's family and friends; it might include all the reciprocal visiting to settle matters; it would include the baking and distribution of the invitational bread without which one cannot have a wedding; it would include all the arrangements with the church and civil authorities; and, finally, it would culminate with the four days of fiesta.

In his article on Subanun religion Frake is concerned essentially with criteria for ethnographic adequacy. He holds that making an ethnographic statement includes at least the following tasks:

> 1. Discovering the major categories of events or *scenes* of the culture. 2. Defining the scenes so that observed interactions, acts, objects, and places can be assigned to their proper scenes as roles, routines, paraphernalia, and settings. 3. Stating the distribution of scenes with respect to one another, that is, providing instructions for anticipating or planning for scenes (1964:112).

Here Frake argues for defining major categories of events and

12

thus is referring to categories which have meaning for the particular culture. A culture may or may not have a major category that corresponds to "dance event." It is the business of the researcher to discover that by observing and questioning rather than to create arbitrary dance event categories by the imposition of his or her own definitions or perceptions.

It may prove useful to proceed further to something that Kealiinohomoku has called dance culture. She defines this as

> an entire configuration, rather than just a performance . . . the implicit as well as explicit aspects of the dance and its reasons for being; the entire conception of the dance within the larger culture, both on a diachronic basis through time and on a synchronic basis of the several parts occurring at the same time (1974a:99).

It remains only to go one more step, as does Merriam, and conclude that "dance is culture and culture is dance" and the "entity of dance is not separable from the anthropological concept of culture" (1974:17). This is the great strength of the anthropological approach to dance. It is the only way of measuring the true significance of dance in any group or society because it is the only approach that looks at the totality into which dance fits. The difficulty is, of course, that in order to say anything at all about dance other than impressionistic statements one has to analyze it, that is, separate it from the rest of culture, as Merriam says, "take the phenomenon to pieces in the hope of finding out what makes it tick" (1974:18). It is hoped that this can be accomplished without doing violence to the phenomenon.

Related to this process of separating the threads that comprise the fabric of culture, and related also to the dance event, is the problem of determining the significance of dance in any particular society or culture. It is obvious that not all aspects of culture are given equal weight. As Benedict observed in 1934, there exists a metaphorical arc of possibilities from which each culture selects. Some cultures give prominence to the dance just

13

as others puzzle endlessly over the complexities of a segmentary lineage system. It has been suggested that dance is "most significant in societies that are least literate, i.e., non-literate" and further that "dance functions in some cultures, with as broad a spectrum of functions as the written word includes for others" (Snyder 1974:213, 214). I would amend this to say that I perceive differences in *kinds* of dance and in the *functions* of dance within literate and nonliterate societies but that I cannot see a difference in signficance that is correlated with the presence or absence of literacy. Why it is that some societies give a prominent role to the dance while others do not, I do not think we can say at this point. What we can do is to note the differing emphases and document the differing functions.

This leads, of course, to the question of how much attention the anthropologist should pay to the dance in any society or culture. Kaeppler has noted that "an adequate description of a culture should place the same emphasis on dance as that given it by the members of that society" (1967b:iii). This is a good guide and true up to a point. That point may, however, be crucial if one happens to be dealing with a society which does not always articulate the significance of different aspects of their culture. So let us turn once more to Frake:

> To describe a culture, then, is not to recount the events of a society but to specify what one must know to make those events maximally probable. The problem is not to state what someone did but to specify the conditions under which it is culturally appropriate to anticipate that he, or persons occupying his role, will render an equivalent performance. This conception of cultural description implies that an ethnography should be a theory of cultural behavior in a particular society, the adequacy of which is to be evaluated by the ability of a stranger to the culture . . . to use the ethnography's statements as instructions for appropriately anticipating the scenes of a society. I say "appropriately anticipate" rather than "predict" because a failure of an ethnographic statement to predict correctly does not necessarily imply descriptive inadequacy as long as the members of the de-

14

scribed society are as surprised by the failure as is the ethnographer. The test of descriptive adequacy must always refer to informants' interpretations of events, not simply to the occurrence of events (1964:112).

Consideration of the Zapotec wedding once more may clarify some of these points. We include dance in our ethnographic description of this scene because a stranger who might have to render a performance of the wedding would have to know that particular dances in specific sequences are necessary to the wedding scene. Using our account which lists the *mediu xhiga, sones,* and *piezas* as dances that are crucial, the uninitiated can "appropriately anticipate" what will occur. Cultural knowledge would have predicted that, in spite of a tropical rainstorm which blew up just at the onset of the *mediu xhiga* at a wedding held in the open, the *mediu xhiga* would continue until all the pottery vessels had been bought and subsequently broken. Both the stranger and the Zapotec would have been suprised had the scene gone otherwise.

It is equally important to remark on the nonoccurrence of dance in those situations where it should occur because this gives clues as to its importance relative to other phenomena. For example, it is customary for Zapotec matrons to dominate the dancing of *sones* at the annual function of the particular society in which they hold membership. It is also a cultural "rule" that one does not dance at all if a close relative has died within the past forty days or longer depending upon the closeness of the relationship. In 1974 Porfirio Pineda, one of the pillars of Zapotec society, died. The forty-day period had just passed when the annual function of the society to which the prominent Pinedas belong was held. The close relatives of Don Porfirio went to the dance because the social norms required their attendance, but they did not participate in the dancing of *sones* because of those same norms. This allows us to make the statement that the dancing of *sones* is somewhat less important in the hierarchy of cultural imperatives than is observing the

15

proper mourning behavior for a close relative. Again, knowing this allows us to anticipate appropriately a cultural scene. And, to answer the question I posed above, if dance is part of the scenes of any society or culture, then the researcher must include it in his ethnographic description simply because without it one cannot anticipate an appropriate performance of those scenes.

Thus far I have spoken primarily, although implicitly for the most part, about the study of dance in specific cultures or societies. This is in one sense paralleling one of the earliest and perhaps most basic emphases that characterizes the field of anthropology, that is, the emphasis on descriptive ethnography. Briefly, that is the area of anthropology which concerns itself primarily with the description of a single culture at a time. Initially these were non-Western cultures as well as preliterate ones. If, however, we are concerned with making generalizing statements and building theory, then description of single units is only the first step of the process. This leads us to comparison of cultures or of dance styles. Because anthropology is the study of man, it has necessarily broadened its horizons to include Western society, industrialized society, and urban society. This allows us within the scope of anthropology to pursue the study of the dance culture of all kinds of societies, so that we may with equal legitimacy observe the dance of the Australian aborigine, the classical tradition of Bharata Natyam, the pigeon wings and polkas of the California gold rush miners, and the minuets of the colonial Virginia planters. Just as Kurath has been the pioneer in so many aspects of dance study, so she was in pioneering this broad approach to dance. In 1960 she wrote:

> Any dichotomy between ethnic dance and art dance dissolves if one regards dance ethnology, not as a description or reproduction of a particular kind of dance, but as an approach toward, and a method of, eliciting the place of dance in human life—in a word, as a branch of anthropology (p. 250).

16

❧ 2 ❧

THE
ANTHROPOLOGICAL
PERSPECTIVE

ONE MAY APPROACH the phenomenon of dance in many ways. The performer enjoys it for the opportunity it provides to master mind and body, to feel a sense of physical release and well-being, and to take pleasure in the camaraderie between performers and between performers and audience. From the other side one may come to dance as a spectator enjoying it for its capacity to entertain, to move, to banish anxiety, or to reaffirm the unity of the community. Looking at the literature on dance, we are at once struck by the wealth of material written about dance from each of these points of view: in the first instance we have accounts of what dance does to and for a person as well as reflections about the role of dance; in the second we have the volumes of dance criticism.

If, on the other hand, we wish to approach dance as one aspect of human behavior inextricably bound up with all those aspects that make up the unity we call culture, then we must approach it as students of humankind, that is, as anthropologists. This by no means excludes the possibility of experiencing dance as either performer or spectator. Indeed, these two viewpoints are incorporated in the anthropological approach. Kaeppler (1967b:32) argues that in order to notate dance accurately, "it is helpful (indeed almost necessary) for the notator to be able to perform the movements himself in order to analyze exactly what the various parts of the body are doing and in what sequence they are done." Performing dances in another culture is also an excellent way of eliciting aesthetic judgments as those native to the dance tradition correct, criticize, or praise your performance. Additionally, it is a way of "storing" the form of dances until you can record them in some more permanent form. A danger inherent in this last use of performing ability is the fact that one's own cultural biases for movement and posture tend to leak and eventually color how one performs other dance traditions. I should say at this point that performing ability is not a requisite skill. It is doubtful that Radcliffe-Brown had ever danced other than an occasional waltz but this lack of familiarity did not prevent him from describing Andaman Island dance so precisely that the reader of his ethnography can reconstruct the dance movements with little difficulty.

The spectator's view of dance is quite in accord with an anthropologist's normal mode of operation. The oldest and most frequently used anthropological technique is that of participant-observation. The term is eminently descriptive of what anthropologists do in the field. They participate in the life of the society in which they are living and they observe it. The proportion of participating to observing varies from anthropologist to anthropologist, and depends upon such factors as the personality of the anthropologist, the characteristics of the host culture, and the particular focus of the research. In my own case Zapotec women were particularly insistent (becoming more so the longer I was among them) that I participate in

Zapotec society doing all the things that a Zapotec matron does: dance, speak Zapotec, go to fiestas, and so on. Once they ascertained that I was not in danger of harming either myself or them through ignorance (see Wagner, 1975), then I was incorporated into their social system. This meant a gradual switch from mostly observing to mostly participating. Participating certainly did not hinder my research, and in some regards it enhanced it. It was particularly valuable with regard to Zapotec dance since almost all dancing takes place either under a sun shade or at night, making it difficult to use film to record dance movement.

A qualitative difference exists, however, between performing and viewing dance impressionistically and treating dance as an object of anthropological inquiry. It is this anthropological perspective that is the subject of this chapter.

Dance has met various fates at the hands of anthropologists over the past one hundred years. Speaking very broadly, we can identify five approaches popular at different times which have dealt quite differently with dance. In chronological order they are 1) the evolutionary approach, 2) the culture trait approach, 3) the culture and personality and culture configuration approach, 4) the problem-oriented approach in complex and plural societies, and 5) the approach that focuses on dance as a unique phenomenon.

Evolutionists on both sides of the Atlantic, who posited a series of stages through which all societies progressed, viewed dance as an essential part of primitive culture. As might be expected, they also held that primitive dance was just as rudimentary and lacking in symmetry and grace as the rest of primitive culture. Most dancing by primitives was thought to be associated with ritual, which in turn was seen as marking every important aspect of life. One has an image of primitive man weighed down by the awful burden of ritual, unable to take, or dance, a step without it. Sir James Frazer documented dance in various eras and locations as being part of homeopathic magic rites; the latter, he suggests, belongs to an early stage of evolution. He tells us, for example, that in Transylvania dancers leap high in the air in order to make the crops grow tall; elsewhere women jump over newly planted crops to insure the latter's fertility; among the Omaha Indians the Buffalo Society held rainmaking rites which involved spilling containers of water. Similar to this view is the one that Martha Beckwith presents in her comparison of Moqui and Kwakiutl dances. She speaks of the imitative use of dance to bring about a desired result, in this case the acquisition of power:

> Formal dances among primitive people are generally dramatic representations in which spirits and the heroic dead are believed actually to take part. The impression depends upon the belief that by imitating the acts of a person or animal, one becomes to some degree imbued with the spirit of that being. By imitating, therefore, the acts performed by the heroes and supernatural beings of the spirit world, one may obtain some of their mysterious power (1906-1907:79).

Edward Tylor associated possession dances with a primitive state of religion:

> Thus, in the religion of uncultured races, the phenomenon of being "struck" holds so recognized a position that imposters will even counterfeit it. . . . Such descriptions of people possessed carry us far back in the history of the human mind, showing modern man still in ignorant sincerity producing the very fits and swoons to which for untold ages savage tribes have given religious import (1958:506-507).

Many of the early anthropologists and scholars in America dealt with the American Indian. By and large their view was that the Indian represented an early stage in the evolutionary schema. Dances of these people would predictably be primitive and integral to their culture. We also find the sentiment that as people progressed to the next stages their dances would be abandoned as a form of exercise not befitting civilized or rational man. One scholar holding such a view was Henry Schoolcraft, who was also responsible for the collecting of much dance data during the last half of the nineteenth century. He composed and sent out a questionnaire in 1847 to all persons who might conceivably be knowledgeable about American Indians. Because he regarded dance as an essential trait of primitive cultures, Schoolcraft included questions on dance in his questionnaire. His feelings about American Indian dance are aptly expressed in the following selection:

> Dancing is both an amusement and a religious observance, among the American Indians, and is known to constitute one of the most widespread traits in their manners and customs. It is accompanied, in all cases, with singing, and, omitting a few cases, with the beating of time on instruments. . . . It is believed to be the ordinary mode of expressing intense passion, or feeling on any subject, and it is a custom which has been preserved in, with the least variation, through all the phases of their history, and probably exists among the remote tribes, precisely at this time, as it did in the era of Columbus. It is observed to be the last thing abandoned by bands and individuals, in their progress to civilization and Christianity. So true is this, that it may be regarded as one of the best practical proofs of their advance, to find the native instruments and music thrown by, and the custom abandoned (1851:221-22).

In the same year Lewis Henry Morgan, in his book on the League of the Iroquois, expressed much the same feelings as Schoolcraft when he commented:

> These amusements [music and dance] of our primitive inhabitants are not, in themselves, devoid of interest, although they indicate a tendency of mind unbefitting rational men (1962, orig. 1851:289-90).

The end of the nineteenth century and beginning of the twentieth brought a reaction against evolutionism in both America and Europe. In Europe the search began for general laws of society which would explain all the particular manifestations that one saw of societies around the world. For many, represented best by Radcliffe-Brown, the key to understanding single societies and to understanding society in general was social structure. All other aspects of society were ranked after structure in terms of importance. Dance was one of those aspects ranked rather far down the list of priorities, so we find relatively few descriptions of dance from early adherents of this school.

In America, in contrast, the emphasis had shifted from the view that held that all societies and cultures progressed through the same series of stages to one which said that each society and culture was the result of a unique combination of history and environment. This was a view that encouraged the culture trait approach. Followers of this approach collected information about all cultural traits rather than selecting a small number which were identified as more significant than the others. Dance study fared quite well in this atmosphere. Some of the tenets of this school are revealed clearly in statements made about the dance; in particular, the belief which saw all traits as being important, and that which saw each culture as being a unique combination of traits and circumstances. Boas, for example, emphasized the importance of dance in Kwakiutl society:

> Song and dance accompany all the events of Kwakiutl life . . . and they are an essential part in the culture of the people. . . . Although there are expert performers, everyone is obliged to take part in the singing and dancing, so that the separation between performer and audience that we find in our modern society does not occur in more primitive society such as that represented by the Kwakiutl Indians (1944:10).

Leslie Spier argued for the uniqueness of cultures when he spoke of various manifestations of the Sun Dance:

> The (various) sun dances are not merely aggregates of diffused elements: the ideas locally injected to integrate the whole and

the rituals originated have transformed them into something unique. How each tribe has made the ceremony peculiarly its own cannot be determined for want of precise historical data. But an approach is possible by recasting the question: in how far does the sun dance conform to preexisting ceremonial patterns? (*in* Mead and Bunzel, 1960:392; from Spier, 1921:505).

Along with the view that every culture was unique in some respect went the related belief that each culture should be valued for itself. The cultural relativism was, of course, also applied to the dances of cultures, thereby presenting an attitude very different from that voiced by the evolutionists. Paul Radin articulated this changed attitude in a statement about the Medicine Dance of the Winnebago:

> In other words, the Medicine Dance from the viewpoint of its leaders at least, was a drama depicting the ideal life and depicting it in terms of a myth from which all the coarser implications of its episodes had been completely obliterated. Such a highly artificial drama can manifestly represent the achievement only of men who have thought deeply on the meaning of life, who possessed the artistic skill to articulate their vision and leisure in which to do it, not to mention an audience that was willing to accept it (1957:305).

Related to the culture trait approach was the defining of culture areas. Aboriginal America was described in terms of areas that had coherence based on similarity of various culture traits. People like Clark Wissler and Alfred Kroeber looked at various items of material culture and belief systems and plotted concentrations of similar items. Based on these concentrations, they began speaking of American Indians in terms of culture areas. Dance was one trait frequently used to help define these areas.[1]

A particularly important kind of change in terms of impact upon both Indians and non-Indians were the several revitalization movements that swept America in the nineteenth century. Dance was a key element in movements such as the ghost dance,

23

grass dance, and peyote movement. Partially because of fear of uprisings and lack of information, the Bureau of American Ethnology sent James Mooney to document the ghost dance. Mooney recorded the ghost dance movement in all its complexity. He saw as well the resemblance between the ghost dance and other revitalization movements both in its general social and historical outlines and in the type of dance that characterized it:

> What tribe or nation has not had its golden age, before Pandora's box was loosed, when women were nymphs and dryads and men were gods and heroes? And when the race lies crushed and groaning beneath an alien yoke, how natural is the dream of a redeemer, an Arthur, who shall return from exile or awake from some long sleep to drive out the usurper and win back for his people what they have lost. The hope becomes a faith and the faith becomes the creed of priests and prophets, until the hero is a god and the dream a religion, looking to some great miracle of nature for its culmination and accomplishment. The doctrines of the Hindu avatar, the Hebrew Messiah, the Christian millennium, and the Hesûnanin of the Indian Ghost dance are essentially the same, and have their origin in a hope and longing common to all humanity (1965:1; orig. 1892-93).

And in speaking of the dance form at a later point, Mooney says:

> As to the dance itself, with its scenes of intense excitement, spasmodic action, and physical exhaustion even to unconsciousness, such manifestations have always accompanied religious upheavals among primitive peoples, and are not entirely unknown among ourselves (*in* Mead and Bunzel, 1960:263).

With the influence of Freud and psychoanalysis in the early 1920s, anthropology in the United States took a new direction. The Culture and Personality school stands as an exemplar of the change in anthropology. Abandoned were the concerns with historical factors and with trait lists. Description was im-

24

portant only insofar as it illuminated theoretical concerns. Rather than being unique agglomerations of traits and history, cultures were seen through the lens of pattern and configuration. Ruth Benedict's *Patterns of Culture*, published in 1934, typifies these concerns. She posits an arc of elements from which all cultures select. Cultures then combine these elements in certain ways so that the result is a configuration. Because of limited possibilities for combinations and elements, certain patterns are repeated over and over. Also, cultures can be characterized according to psychological set. Benedict speaks in the very broadest sense of two psychological types, Apollonian and Dionysian. To illustrate she describes the Hopi as being essentially Apollonian and the Kwakiutl and Dobu as being Dionysian.

Dances were no longer recorded as a matter of course because they were cultural manifestations without the recording of which one's description of any given culture would be incomplete. The number and quality of dance descriptions fall sharply with this shift in focus within anthropology. In culture and personality studies, dance was mentioned only if it was directly pertinent to the psychological state of individuals within the culture being studied. Margaret Mead's *Coming of Age in Samoa*, first published in 1928, is an excellent example. Mead talks about Samoan dance because in Samoan society, where conformity is the norm, dance provides the one area where individualism is tolerated:

> The significance of the dance in the education and socialization of Samoan children is two-fold. In the first place it effectively offsets the rigorous subordination in which children are habitually kept. . . . The second influence of the dance is its reduction of the threshold of shyness (1967:117-18; orig. 1928).

In studies of this kind, dance was discussed only if it contributed to an explanation of the personality structure of individuals within cultures or to psychologically oriented explanations of cultural patterns. The form of the dance was sketched briefly and in very general terms, if at all.

The notable exception to the overall pattern of psychologically-oriented research is the extensive body of literature on dissociational states and the dance that frequently accompanies them. Dance, both in form and in context, looms large in many of these studies. It is still viewed as a universal cultural phenomenon; we can say that the habit of looking for pattern above the level of individual societies that characterized the culture and personality school remained to distinguish these later studies as well. The comments of Erika Bourguignon are relevant here:

> Ecstatic dance . . . represents a vital form of human expression in the context of particular, larger, cultural wholes. It must be seen in each instance within that cultural whole, and yet we must be aware that it represents not merely a particular local invention, but a local utilization of a universal human capacity which has been used in many societies throughout human history (1968:60).

Anthropologists began expanding their horizons after the 1930s to include the study of urban settings, plural societies, and Western industrialized societies. This was a gradual process of reeducating both scholars and the public, who carried in their minds an image of the anthropologist as that person who studied the exotic, the faraway, the primitive. So much was this attitude part of some persons that they began to fear the day when this kind of subject matter would have disappeared from the face of the earth. Malinowski expressed what preyed upon the minds of many when he wrote in 1922:

> Ethnology is in the sadly ludicrous, not to say tragic, position, that at the very moment when it begins to put its workshop in order . . . the material of its study melts away with hopeless rapidity (p. xv).

The new kinds of studies did not aim at simple description of small, relatively homogeneous situations, nor did they focus upon social structure as the key to unlock a treasure chest of general laws of society. Neither were they interested in cataloguing societies according to personality types. Anthropological investigations now were rapidly becoming problem-oriented. Many dealt with problems brought about by urbanization or industrialization. Others focused upon situations where formerly isolated groups were exposed to one another and were forced to develop strategies for coping with a radically different social setting. New methods appeared to deal with the change of subject matter, two of which were situational analysis and social drama. The first is a concept that isolates "temporally and spatially bounded series of events . . . from the on-going flow of social life" (Garbett, 1970:215). It is useful, as Van Velsen has noted, "as a method of integrating variations, exceptions, and accidents into descriptions of regularities. . . . Situational analysis, with its emphasis on process, might therefore be particularly suited for the study of unstable and non-homogeneous societies" (1967:143).

The method of focusing upon drama is closely linked to that of situational analysis. Dramatic events range. from a heated quarrel in the fish market to the pomp surrounding the opening of a new bridge to actual dramatic, dance, or musical performances. What all social drama shares is an intensification or exaggeration of ordinary behavior. These kinds of events allow an outsider to see values stated forcefully. On this basis one may then begin to say something about priorities with regard to values and rules for behavior; one may order the cultural rules. Dance frequently is the central activity in events of this nature. An example from the Zapotec of Juchitán will illustrate the illumination and ordering of cultural rules that one might observe in a dance situation.

Every year the Zapotec of Juchitán send a delegation of dancers to the Guelaguetza in Oaxaca City, the state capital. Delegations from the various indigenous groups in the state perform traditional dances and music on the occasion of the Guelaguetza. The Juchitán delegation in the summer of 1972 consisted of twelve dancers, six women and six men. Selection of the dancers to represent Juchitán is always based on a number of factors. The women tend to come from the older, wealthier families. More specifically, they tend to come from families who are currently aligned with the political powers in the city. Dancing ability is also a factor, and, generally speaking, those chosen are among the better dancers in the city. Men are selected after the women have been chosen, and their selection is primarily a function of friendship with the women dancers, willingness to take part, and dancing ability.

Once the dancers have been chosen, rehearsals begin. It is one of these rehearsals that I offer as an example of a dramatic event. The dancers were rehearsing the *fandango,* an open couple dance that is regarded as one of the most traditional of the Zapotec dances. The music and the dance alternate between fast and slow sections. The beginning of each section is marked by an exchange of places between the man and the woman. As the *fandango* progressed, it became apparent that two couples were changing places when the change in music occured while four couples were beginning the exchange two measures before the change in the music. María Luisa (all names have been changed), an older dancer who has frequently been a delegate to the Guelaguetza and who is the acknowledged expert on the matter of dancing, corrected her young cousin, Elena, who was a member of one of the two couples. According to all the cultural rules about deference to age and expert knowledge, Elena should have accepted the correction. Instead, she contended that she and Julia were correct. Furthermore, she said that she was following the example of Beatrice, María Luisa's grandmother and a woman regarded as one of the finest dancers in Juchitán.

Elena became more and more excited and angry, and the rest of the dancers reacted more or less according to Zapotec standards of behavior. The men took themselves off to one corner of the courtyard, where they ignored the proceedings, smoking and talking among themselves. Julia from time to time supported Elena by comments and nods since Julia, too, would lose face if María Luisa's correction was accepted. Pilar, the second oldest woman and best friend of María Luisa, voiced her support of María Luisa's opinion. Antonia and Teresa stood to one side waiting for the outcome but prepared, if necessary, to support María Luisa since both Antonia and Teresa came from families with social status lower than that of María Luisa's family. Their families receive favors from the more prestigious family of María Luisa in return for support.

Everyone was embarrassed. When it became obvious that Elena only became more vocally adamant when subjected to pressure in front of the others, María Luisa and Pilar took her aside. This action was prompted by two Zapotec cultural values. One value holds that public disagreements and expressions of emotion should be limited to certain ritual kinds of situations. The second, and perhaps more crucial on this occasion, holds that one's allegiance belongs first to family. The women of the delegation represented two of the oldest families in Juchitán who have a long tradition of rivalry. One family, the Gómez, was represented by María Luisa, Pilar, Elena, and indirectly by Antonia and Teresa since their families are regarded as clients of the Gómez. The other family, the Martínez, was represented only by Julia. Her position was strengthened, however, by the fact that her cousin was the municipal president and she herself was the director of the Casa de la Cultura, an institution whose purpose is to celebrate Zapotec tradition. Nonetheless, the branch of the Martínez family represented by Julia was regarded by the Gómez as being relative newcomers to the city and therefore none of its members could be regarded as an authority on Zapotec tradition. Dance, and especially the *fandango,* is one of the most significant items of Zapotec tradition.

In the whispered dialogue Elena was reminded of all the great Gómez dancers in an attempt to prod her into doing the appropriate thing, namely acknowledging the Gómez superiority as represented by its oldest member on that occasion, María Luisa. Elena stubbornly refused. She said she would not be satisfied until Beatrice herself supported changing places two measures before the musical change. This put an end to the afternoon's rehearsal. Gómez and Gómez supporters went to consult Beatrice. Everyone agreed to meet for another rehearsal within the next few days.

The case was presented to Beatrice by María Luisa, speaking very calmly and quietly, and by Elena, hotly defending herself. Beatrice asked them each to do the *fandango,* and she then supported María Luisa's version as being the correct one. At that point Elena accused Beatrice of having done the same version as Elena had just done on the last festive occasion of the Gómez family. No Zapotec likes to discomfit another Zapotec directly, so, rather than saying herself that Elena was wrong, Beatrice turned to her own daughter Vicenta (also María Luisa's mother and Elena's aunt) and asked her what she remembered about dancing on that occasion. Vicenta agreed with Beatrice that the latter had done the *fandango* just as the Gómez have always done it, changing two measures before the music. Elena could no longer maintain her position in the face of the combined age, authority, and numerical advantage. She went huffily to her room, too young still to accept defeat gracefully.

At the next rehearsal the Gómez presented a united front for their version of the *fandango.* Julia argued for her version tacitly using the weight of her position with the Casa de la Cultura. She quickly abandoned her cause when it was suggested that all the dancers adopt Julia's version since the Gómez version admittedly was much more difficult, and the object was to have dances that all the dancers could perform well.

A postscript is necessary at this point. One month later I was dancing the *fandango* with yet another Gómez woman. Two measures before the musical change, I started to cross over into her position, at which point she informed me that I was to wait until the music changed. Many observations and questions later, it became obvious to me that both versions were acceptable variants of the *fandango*. The cultural values being upheld on the occasion of the rehearsal were those of Gómez superiority and necessity to show family allegiance and unity. That Elena was the youngest Gómez involved in the dispute made the resolution simpler because age brings with it respect and authority. Youth is accorded little of either. Elena's protest was the protest of youth against age and authority. That she made it in a public situation where a rival family was involved caused the result to be as firm as it was inevitable.

Dance and drama seemed to acquire added significance in the kinds of plural societies that anthropologists had begun to investigate in the late 1950s. They were used in different ways from the ways that members of nonplural societies used them. For one thing dance, and to a lesser extent drama and music, was an excellent vehicle for communicating ideas about one's own identiy as well as for parodying the identity of others. J.C. Mitchell's (1956) study of the Kalela dance phenomenon in the African Copperbelt is one of the first to view dance in this way. In their dances and songs Kalela dancers praise their own tribe, the Bisa, while satirizing the numerous other tribes living in the same area. Just recently Ranger (1975) had documented many dances that served as central foci for revitalization-like movements throughout East Africa. James Peacock (1968) concentrated on the dance and drama of Java to understand how modernization was being effected in that country. Charles Keil (1966) called attention to the use of blues music in urban settings.

The most recent trend in the anthropological study of dance views dance as dance rather than solely for what it may tell us about something else. Most of the studies focus upon the form of dance and could be said to take a symbolic, structural, or semiotic approach. The important point to be made about these studies, varied as they are in terms of approach, dance type, and period, is that they contend that dance has unique qualities. It is one aspect of culture among many but it functions in a distinctive manner and it is vital to record it or its

31

functions in terms of its unique qualities. That is, dance is *not* the same as language nor does it function in the same way; it is not identical with other forms of expressive behavior though at times it may appear to be used similarly. Dance may sometimes fill the same functional slot as other culture traits, but because it has features which distinguish it from all other traits, it will fill the slot in a different way. The new studies scrutinize dance as a phenomenon in its own right. Because dance is inseparable from the people who do it, ultimately we must return the phenomenon to its context. When we do return it, however, it will be with a much better understanding of its complex properties.

Thus far I have discussed the fate of dance within the context of the last one hundred years of anthropological research. I have also suggested that there is something distinctive about the anthropological approach to dance which separates it from all other approaches. Let us look, then, at these procedures which, in order, form the basis of the anthropological method, observation, description, and analysis.

Unless the anthropologist is working solely from written materials, the research must begin with observation. I have already indicated in Chapter 1 something of what happens in the process of observing when I spoke of the human tendency to categorize. Confronted by a foreign culture, we automatically try to bring some order into the chaos, to make some sense of what is strange and unfamiliar. In doing this we look for commonalities or links between a strange custom and something out of our own cultural inheritance. This is an essential kind of adaptation which allows us to survive outside our normal environment. Lamentably, however, it does distort what we observe. We draw parallels where perhaps there are none, and we categorize phenomena on the basis of perhaps misleading superficial characteristics.

An area that suffers most often from this kind of survival-oriented distortion, and that will be familiar to the reader, is language. In most field situations the first stressful confrontation for the researcher is the one between himself or herself and an unfamiliar language, usually a non-Indo-European one. An instinctive response to hearing a totally unintelligible language is to make it more familiar and more manageable by trying to discern the divisions between words, thereby isolating units of meaning. Then one must assign the proper meaning to each of the units one has so laboriously isolated. Finally, the now meaningful units must go back together to make sense out of the whole phrase or set of phrases. If one's own native language is English, one then tries to fit the new language into the structure of English and spends much time looking for subjects, verbs, and objects, not to mention the familiar verb tenses. None of them may, in fact, exist in the other language, but more often than not we derive considerable comfort from having looked for them.

We tend to do the same thing when we observe an unfamiliar dance for the first time. We search for units of a size that we can remember. That particular size most comfortable for us is, of course, a size familiar to us from our own dance traditions. For example, the meaningful units in classical ballet are the basic steps, all of which are named and all of which fit within the bounds of certain phrase lengths. Compared to the sizes of meaningful units in the *huapangos* of Veracruz, Mexico, the ballet units are much shorter. It seems quite probable that unit sizes for dance movement vary considerably from one culture to another, although no systematic research has yet been done in this area. So, once again, we do damage to the reality of the unfamiliar language, dance, or culture by our seemingly inescapable tendency to try to make it familiar. The longer one spends in the unfamiliar situation, the more likely it is that this initial distortion will be corrected. In other words, the problem of distortion is not insurmountable. It also becomes less problematical if one is aware of the danger and can take measures to neutralize its effects.

Description follows from observation. Just as there is some distortion involved in the process of observation, so there is the inevitable distortion in the process of describing observations. Unavoidably we are selective about what we observe due to a combination of cultural constraints, both ours and theirs. A pig slaughter may not be on your "must" list of things to see, just as the members of the other culture may never extend an invitation to a funeral if it is the kind of event that only close family attend.

When we commit to writing our description of what we have seen, we rarely, regardless of our intentions, record it in its entirety. In the beginning of our field work we do not know what is significant and what is trivial; to do justice to our observations, we try to record them all in detail. As our familiarity grows, we can afford to be somewhat more selective. For example, after attending twenty weddings we should know what the diagnostic features of weddings are and then we may need only to record deviations from what is normal. It is not necessary to notate the *mediu xhiga,* for example, for every Zapotec wedding we attend. We notate it only if there is something out of the ordinary about it. Just as it is the factor of repeated exposure that erases much potential distortion, so it is repeated descriptions of similar events and phenomena that help to insure fidelity to the reality of the unfamiliar culture. The description of dance involves special problems which will be discussed at length in the next chapter.

Analysis of our descriptions based on observations is the final step in the process of the study of one society or culture. It is in this stage that we move furthest perhaps from the reality of the situation as those native to it know it. Up to this point we should have drawn relatively few conclusions about what is going on and the meaning of events, behavior, and values. Now it is time to sit back, reflect upon our descriptions and the interpretations offered by those native to the culture, and try to produce an analysis that is most compatible with the three levels at which all phenomena may be seen: 1) the actual behavior, 2) the natives' interpretation of the behavior, and 3) the analyst's interpretation. It is rare that there is a perfect match between all three. The reasons for this are easily understood. We know, for example, that there is no necessary causal relationship between a person's attitudes or values and his or her behavior. A Zapotec may tell us, for example, that the traditional *sones* are always danced barefoot. Our own observation tells us that only lower-class women or very old women ever dance them barefoot because going barefoot is an indication of a lower social status. Why have people said that they are danced barefoot? Because this is a cultural ideal dating from a time when everyone did, in fact, dance without shoes. To further complicate matters, occasions do arise when women of high social standing will dance barefoot. The occasions are usually those where there is a desire to emphasize a true Zapotec identity.

The lack of fit between stated ideals and actual behavior should not cause great concern. The areas of *non*correspondence are important because they tell us something about the culture we might otherwise miss. The fact that this happens all the time is simply another argument for checking our observations against what we are told, by speaking to people in a wide range of statuses, and by using written sources as a check.

A second factor which produces a mismatch between what goes on at the three levels is the fact that there is very seldom any one person in the society who has access to enough information to be able to see the whole picture. This means that what any one person tells us is skewed because of the particular position he or she occupies. Someone from the Zapotec lower class views the city of Juchitán as being composed of insiders and outsiders first of all. Second, the insiders, or Zapotec, are divided into two groups, the rich and the poor. The outsiders fall mostly into the rich category. That same city viewed by a middle- or upper-class Zapotec is divided quite differently. The same two large categories are the primary basis of division, insiders and outsiders. Each of these two groups is further divided, however, into three social classes each: lower, middle, and upper.

Anthropologists who do their job well should have more information than any one person in the society though, of course, it is of a qualitatively different kind. It is up to the researcher then to explain the workings of that society with reference to the particular problem chosen to be resolved. It is not part of the work to reconcile all the differences and reduce them to some common denominator but rather to note them and then to explain why they exist. To attempt to eliminate the contradictions is to return to an older idealistic and inaccurate view of society where every part had its contribution to make to the functioning of the whole society, which remained in a happy state of equilibrium.

Observation, description, and analysis are the building blocks of anthropological research. From here, the next step is that of comparison, which allows us to make more general statements about human society and behavior. Comparison depends on good description and analysis at the level of a single culture or society. If these are inadequate then the results of the comparison will also be inadequate. It is possible to compare several kinds of phenomena. One may choose to compare whole societies, but just as frequently specific aspects of societies are compared. Dance may be compared just as any other aspect of human behavior is. In Robert Textor's *Cross-Cultural Summary* (1967), for example, there is a listing for exhibitionistic dancing. If we look at the listing, we can see which of the cultures for which data are available have this kind of dancing and which do not. We can also see what other cultural traits are associated with exhibitionistic dancing and how strong the association is. For instance, cultures with exhibitionistic dancing also tend to have no belief in the uncleanness of women and to emphasize an invidious display of wealth (cf. Textor 1967, FC475). This illustrates one possible kind of comparison using dance material. Chapter 6 is devoted entirely to comparison as it relates to the study of dance. Let it suffice for the moment to say that the ultimate purpose of anthropology is to describe and compare the specific and arrive at the general in order to illuminate the phenomenon of human behavior. Otherwise anthropology is simply collecting quaint customs.

Assuming that we include dance as a proper subject for anthropological investigation, then we must insist that dance study conform to the same standards and procedures that anthropologists use in studying other aspects of humankind. We should be observing, describing, analyzing, and comparing dance data. We should be able to talk not only about specific forms and contexts of dance but also about the phenomenon of dance in general. If we survey how anthropologists have viewed dance in the last one hundred years, we see that it is only very recently that we have ventured beyond simple recording of dance phenomena. The time and effort needed to build foundations, when so few are contracted and those few are scattered widely in time and space, is not to be lamented. We have reached the point now that Gertrude Kurath anticipated in an article on research methods, the time for "the conclusions, the theories, the comparisons with dances of other cultures, adjacent or distant, in the light of history" (1974:38).

🖘 3 🖙

METHODS AND
TECHNIQUES

ONE OF THE major reasons that anthropological study
of dance lags behind the discipline of anthropology
itself must surely be the attitude of most anthropologists. They
have defended their neglect of the dance by shrouding it in
mystery, by relegating it to the category of esoterica (about
which it is nice to know something but which is not really essential compared to the more important categories of ethnographic research), and finally by referring to the "difficulty" of
observing and collecting information about the dance in the
first place, and of analyzing and storing it in the second place.
The purpose of this chapter is to remove at least some of the
veils of mystery surrounding the dance and to suggest practical
means for lessening the difficulties of collecting dance data.

As Juana de Laban noted in 1954, "movement is one of the
least explored of all forms of communication when it comes to
making a permanent record of its manifestations" (Laban,
1954:291). We have made some progress since 1954 in our ability to produce permanent records of dance phenomena although the recording of dance is still not a commonplace procedure like, say, the recording of music.

38

Although dance is one of the oldest of the arts, it has had one of the shortest histories in terms of permanent records. An adequate system of dance notation, which is one kind of permanent record, must deal successfully with three different elements: movement through space, movement through time, and the stylistic variations and idiosyncracies that comprise what we may call "performance."

Traditionally, and until quite recently, dance was usually passed on personally from master to pupil or perhaps preserved in folk tradition. The earliest notation for which we have a record dates from two manuscripts from the middle of the fifteenth century found in the municipal archives of Cervera, Catalonia. One of the manuscripts employs abbreviations of the names of steps, in addition to the horizontal and vertical strokes and signs for the beginning and end of dances. These abbreviations include "R" for *reverencia*, "p" for *passo*, "de" for *doble*, and "re" for *represa* (Laban, 1954). This is the earliest example of *symbol substitution*, one of the three main approaches to notating dance.

The most familiar early use of symbol substitution, and the most detailed record of fifteenth- and sixteenth-century dances, is Arbeau's *Orchesography*, published in 1588. Like the earlier manuscripts, it includes descriptions of the *basse* dances, but it also provides notations of other popular dances like the *allemande, branle, courante, gagliarde, gavotte, moresca, pavane,* and *volta*. Arbeau lists and describes all the steps and positions that occur in these dances and then abbreviates the names to the first letter: "R" for *reverence*, "b" for *branle*, "s" for *single*, "d" for *double*, "r" for *reprise*, and so forth. These letters are then placed under the musical note on which the step is to be performed. As long as the number of dance steps remained limited and the floor pattern was uncomplicated, this form of notation was perfectly adequate. Throughout the seventeenth century variations of it appeared from time to time.

With the rise of professional dancing in the early eighteenth century and with the increasing complexity of the new dances, a different approach to notation was introduced. Subsequently labeled *track drawing*, it was first made popular by Raoul Feuillet in his *Chorégraphie ou l'Art de d'écrire la Danse* (1701). Feuillet's innovations were major ones and can be attributed in part to changing styles in the dance. Unlike Arbeau, whose symbols represented *conventional steps*, Feuillet's symbols stood for *basic steps*.[2] In *Chorégraphie*, he begins by describing positions of the feet that are "basic" to all the dances, and he then proceeds to symbols that indicate "steps, jumps and movements of the head, arm, and knee, along with tempo and directional notations" (Laban, 1946:98). Feuillet uses the four corners of the room to indicate the direction in which the dancer is facing, a usage still followed in the classical ballet (see Vaganova, 1963:12). Step symbols are placed alongside a horizontal line; "right" and "left" are indicated by which side of the line the symbols are placed. The line is then arranged so as to show the floor pattern. The correspondence of music and steps is demonstrated by numbering the measures in the musical score and placing the numbers beside the appropriate step symbol (see Figs. 1 and 2).

The important change from conventional step notation to basic step notation reflects certain changes that had occurred in dance events. Dancing as a form of theatrical entertainment was becoming more and more important, and this placed an emphasis upon the professionally trained dancer whose technique was beyond the capabilities of the talented amateur. The establishment of the Academie Royale de Musique under Lully in 1671 is one indication of this change. In the social sphere, dances were no longer composed of predictable sequences of a relatively small number of conventional steps. Frances Rust speaks to this point in her discussion of one of the institutions of Georgian England, the King's Birthnight Ball:

A new dance was always composed for this occasion by the court dancing-master: it was printed in stenochoreographic notation . . . for circulation to other dancing-masters and for sale to the public. Those people hoping to attend, or wishing to give the

40

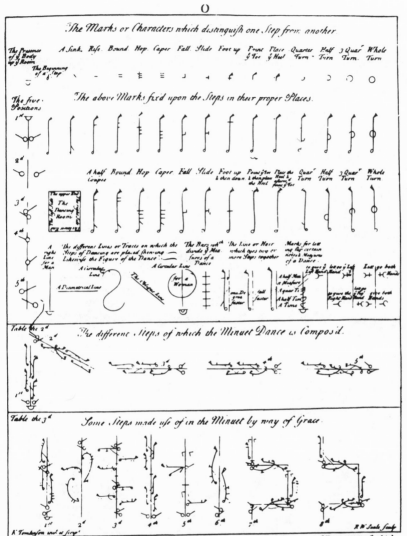

1. Basic notation symbols of Feuillet as used by Kellom Tomlinson in 1735

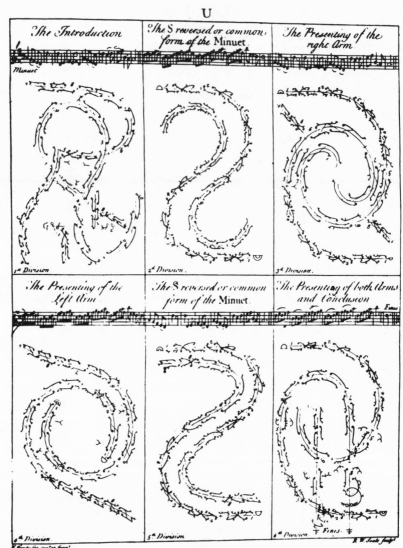

2. Floor plan of a minuet using Feuillet's track-drawing method. From Kellom Tomlinson, 1735

impression that they were going to attend, had to know the new dance. It must be stressed that a particular feature of dancing in the eighteenth century was this individual creation of dances to fit one particular piece of music: one bourrée, for example, could not be danced to the music of another. Sometimes a dance would take on a multiple form, a combination of several dances in one, for example, sarabande-bourrée (1969:59).

Feuillet's notation, with the later refinements of Rameau and Malpied, succeeded in gaining unanimous acceptance by the leading dancing masters of England, France, Italy, Spain, and Germany. Not the least of the incentives was the fact that it allowed dancing masters to recreate each other's choreographies with a minimum of effort. The fact that dance could now be preserved in written form was recognized by writers of the period as well as by the dancing masters. Tomlinson comments in the preface to his book *Six Dances* (1720):

> Our ablest Masters have laboured (not in vain) to Number among other Arts and Sciences, Orchesography, or the Art of Dancing by demonstrative Characters; by which, the various Turns and Movements of the Body, are plainly directed and express'd; which Art is now become equal, and of the same Use, with Notes, etc., in Musick (quoted in Beaumont, 1929:174).

As marked an advance as the Feuillet system was, it was based on a specific style of dance, and so its usefulness came to an end with the demise of that dance style. It was the nineteenth century that saw a completely new approach to dance notation. The new systems were based on the *stick figure,* and new as well was the attempt of some of them to notate movement rather than either conventional or basic steps. This latter innovation meant that the notation systems need not be linked to specific dance tradition. Charles Arthur Saint-Léon, in his *Stenochorégraphie* (1852), is credited with initiating this radical departure from earlier systems. Saint-Léon's stick figures are drawn on a musical staff with steps that remain on

43

the ground being placed on the lines and those done in the air being placed in the spaces. He placed his movement symbols above the musical notes on which the movement was to be performed

Also based on the stick figure was the system devised by Friedrich Zorn and published as *Grammatik der Tanzkunst* in 1887. This outstanding work of the nineteenth century was the result of painstaking study of previous systems, consultations with leading figures in the world of dance, and hours of observation. It is worth quoting Zorn on his decision to use the human figure as a basis for his system:

> It is plain that the use of different symbols by individual choreographs leads to unavoidable ambiguity, and that the only manner in which a script may become universally intelligible and definite is to adopt universal and arbitrary symbols which will not be subject to change, but will remain the same during all time. . . . After carefully considering each one of the systems referred to, the Author has selected for the purpose a sign of the person which corresponds to the anatomical structure of the body. Working upon the principle that this kind of symbol would be intelligible to all nations and would need no translation in any language (as would be the case if letters were used), he has, therefore, evolved a sign that he believes will be perfectly clear (quoted in Shoup, 1951:25).

Modifications and combinations of all three of the approaches to dance notation have appeared in this century. We can apply three basic criticisms to most of the modified and combined notations. They are either too idiosyncratic to be applicable to all types of dance, or too complicated to be easily memorized and used, or too simple to record details of dances with precision (Laban, 1946:117). Three leading notations based on the kind of universal and arbitrary symbols that Zorn felt to be necessary seem to have avoided these pitfalls: *Labanotation, Benesh notation,* and *Effort-Shape*.[3]

Labanotation grew out of the work in Germany of Rudolf

von Laban, whose interests encompassed many of the theatrical arts as well as the relationship of man to machine. His theories of the forms of movement in space (choreutics) and of the qualities of movement (eukinetics) led him to base his notation on human movement in general, rather than on dance movement. Labanotation is therefore theoretically applicable to "any field in which there is a need to record the motions of the human body" (Hutchinson, 1954:5).

At the time it appeared, Laban's system, in addition to the relatively small core of symbols, offered two major innovations: the vertical staff, which was read from bottom to top and clearly showed left and right and front and back; and the varied length of the symbols themselves to denote varying durations of movement. In Europe the new notation rapidly spread among dance scholars, particularly those in the Eastern European countries, and they made slight modifications in the original system. A collection of articles in the *Rad Kongresa Folklorista Jugoslavije* (1958) indicates the state of various notation systems throughout this area in the 1950s. In America Ann Hutchinson, a student of Sigurd Leeder in England, clarified and added to Laban's notation and in 1954 published *Labanotation: The System for Recording Movement.* In Labanotation each symbol carries four different types of information: *the time value, the direction of the movement, the part of the body doing the movement,* and *the level of execution* (see Figs. 3 and 4).

Although Labanotation boasts a great economy of symbols, while at the same time having the capacity to make an "etic" transcription of movement (just as one would make a phonetic transcription of a language using a phonetic alphabet), there are some drawbacks to its use by anthropologists studying dance in the field. Many kinds of ethnic dance require additional notes and symbols outside the regular staff, which often vitiate the original economy of the system. For recording very simple or repetitious dances one may not want such a fine analytical tool. Related to the last and perhaps major disadvantage is that the complexity of any system capable of recording all

45

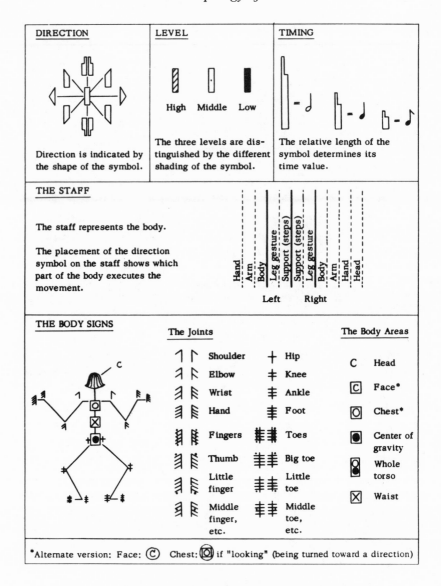

DIRECTION	LEVEL	TIMING
Direction is indicated by the shape of the symbol.	High Middle Low The three levels are distinguished by the different shading of the symbol.	The relative length of the symbol determines its time value.

THE STAFF

The staff represents the body.

The placement of the direction symbol on the staff shows which part of the body executes the movement.

Hand | Arm | Body | Leg gesture | Support (steps) | Support (steps) | Leg gesture | Body | Arm | Hand | Head

Left   Right

THE BODY SIGNS

The Joints

The Body Areas

The Joints			
Shoulder	Hip	C	Head
Elbow	Knee	Face*	
Wrist	Ankle	Chest*	
Hand	Foot	Center of gravity	
Fingers	Toes	Whole torso	
Thumb	Big toe		
Little finger	Little toe	Waist	
Middle finger, etc.	Middle toe, etc.		

*Alternate version: Face: Ⓒ   Chest: if "looking" (being turned toward a direction)

3. Labanotation symbols for direction, level, and timing of movements and symbols for body parts. From Hutchinson, 1954. *Used by permission of the Dance Notation Bureau, New York*

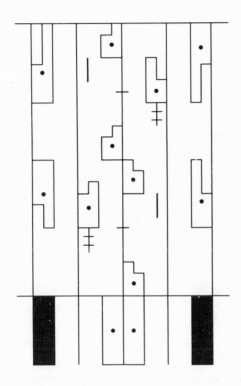

4. A "skip" with natural arm movements in Labanotation. *Drawing by Ronald R. Royce*

distinguishable movements renders it extremely difficult to use to record dance in a field setting if one is seeing the dance for the first time.

Benesh notation was developed in England by Joan and Rudolf Benesh, initially for use in recording ballet choreography. A first form with all the significant features of the later system was created in 1949, some twenty years after Laban had begun work on his movement notation. Briefly, the Benesh system records static positions and the movements preceding them. It avoids repetition by noting only movement and changes in static positions. As a recording device Benesh notation uses a five-line horizontal staff. This becomes a matrix for the human body as seen from the back, so that the reader or notator's right and left sides are the same as those of the dancer. From bottom to top the lines represent the floor, knee, waist, shoulder, and top of the head. Symbols that indicate a position or movement that is level or in line with the body, in front of the body, or behind the body, give a third dimension to the system (see Fig. 5). The advantages of Benesh notation as a field tool are its simplicity, its economy of symbols, and the fact that you do not record unchanging poses (see Fig. 6). It is also sometimes an advantage to have the movement notation in the same format as musical transcription. Although Benesh notation was developed for recording ballet, it is by no means limited to that tradition. It is widely used throughout Europe by individuals working in physical education, medicine, physiotherapy, and industrial time-and-motion studies.

We are indebted to Laban again for the development of a third major system of movement notation widely used today. Like most of us who have more than just a passing interest in movement, Laban began describing movement long before the formulation of any of his notation systems.

Fully a quarter of a century before the first publication of my system, I began to experiment with the idea of writing down movements as one writes words or music. Initially I had nothing

48

—   **LEVEL (with the body)**

| **IN FRONT (of the body)**

•   **BEHIND (the body)**

standing, arms forward   **walking**   **kicking a ball**

5. Benesh notation staff and symbols for level (with the body), in front (of the body), and behind (the body). From Marguerite Causley, *Benesh Movement Notation*, 1967. *Courtesy of the Institute of Choreology, London*

more in mind than to record for my personal use, by a few meaningful scribbles, the steps or gestures I had invented, mainly for my large orchestral dance compositions (1956:11).

His initial system was meant to record both the qualitative and quantitative aspects of movement. As Bartenieff points out, however, this proved too cumbersome, so subsequently he con-

6. A "skip" with natural movements in Benesh notation. *Drawing by Ronald R. Royce*

centrated on the structural content. The first publication of Labanotation in 1927

> describes the sequence of an event in terms of body part, spatial path, transference of weight, and its time value as duration. Its records allow one to study a choreographic work, reconstruct it, and analyze its structural units (Bartenieff *in* Comstock, 1974:180-81).

During World War II Laban carried out efficiency studies for British industry and found that for this type of study it was necessary to focus more intently upon qualitative aspects of movement. *Effort* was the term that Laban used to refer to the qualities of exertion involved in the workers' movements. *Shape* was a concept introduced somewhat later by a colleague, Warren Lamb, which drew largely from the

> affinities of certain effort qualities with specific dimensions of space which were discussed by Laban in his *Choreutics,* a study of space harmony. . . . Thus Effort-Shape became a method of describing changes in movement quality in terms of the kinds of exertions and the kinds of body adaptations in space (Dell, 1970:6-7).

One of the most significant features of Effort-Shape is that unlike the other notation systems, it is concerned with the *quality* of movement as well as with direction, duration, and, to a limited extent, structure.[4] It is quite conceivable that one could have two movements which were identical in terms of *direction, duration,* and *structure* but which conveyed totally different meanings because of differences in the movement *quality.* It is the quality of movement that makes the art of mime come alive, indeed, possible. Consider, for example, Marceau's mime "The Cage." What makes it believable is the strain in the prisoner's hands and arms as he pushes against the invisible walls and the sudden release as he encounters an opening. Perhaps this is because, as Marceau says, "a mime sculptures space while a dancer fills it" (*Dance Magazine,* August 1975, p. 36). Although this capacity may not be appropriate to every problem or instance, it is essential to have a notation system with these capabilities simply because there are whole categories of movement that can be described in no other way without losing their distinctiveness.

The problem today no longer has to do with the capacity for translating movement into words or symbols so that we may talk about it in a meaningful way. We have at least three systems of movement notation which, because they are based on universal and arbitrary symbols, may be applicable to all movement, including dance movement. Any one of these systems would certainly be adequate to the tasks of 1) making a permanent record of an otherwise fleeting phenomenon, 2) providing a way in which choreographies may be included as part of published research, 3) contributing to the establishment of an archive of notated scores that would facilitate and encourage comparative and diachronic studies, and 4) aiding in the structural analysis of dance by virtue of the fact that patterns are more readily discernible in a notated score than in any other kind of description.

No method is wholly adequate for the task of recording dance in the field as it is happening, except perhaps by very experienced notators. A person cannot record steps, spatial arrangement, number and sex of dancers, etc. on viewing a dance only one time in any of these notation systems. Their usefulness comes later when one has the leisure to flesh out rough notes;

51

when one can sit down at a table away from the elements and the crowds and set down one's impressions at one's own pace. If this is done before memories fade and one's own notes begin to seem as if they were written by a total stranger, one will have a convenient permanent record which can then be checked with persons of that dance tradition to discover any errors of omission or embellishment.

Is there, then, any way to record dance on the spot?

The answer is that there are as many ways as there are dance researchers. Almost without exception, people working in the field develop their own shorthand systems of notation suited to the particular dance style with which they are dealing. *Romanotation,* for example, was developed to record Roumanian dance. Consequently, it has the capacity for noting many different kinds of foot movements while having almost no symbols at all for arms, hands, and torso. It works extremely well for Roumanian dance but would be hopelessly inadequate for, say, Tongan dance, which emphasizes movements of the arms and hands. It is precisely this paring down to only the elements one is going to encounter which makes these individual systems useful in the field while rendering them less desirable for making permanent records and of limited utility for comparative purposes.

Given a familiarity with movement in general or dance movement in particular, the individual researcher can devise his or her own means of recording dance in the field. Spending a long enough period of time in one place makes it possible to see dance on many occasions. Ideally, one will be in a situation where it is possible to learn dances and dance style. Actually learning the dances is very important, and it should be attempted if at all practical in a particular field situation. First, by learning the dances well one can record them more easily and accurately at one's own pace. Second, by being criticized one develops a sense of what is important enough in the local style to be valued or disliked. Third, the situation lends itself to questions which are often not appropriate at dance events themselves.

Just as the advent of the wire recorder and the tape recorder was viewed by some as the ultimate solution to the problems of recording music in the field, so has film been viewed as the answer to making a record of dance. But the tape recorder has not rendered music transcription obsolete, and neither is film likely to make dance notation a thing of the past. The truth of the matter is that film and notation complement each other because they have distinct and nonoverlapping uses. Let us now turn our attention to the uses of film.

If film is to contribute in any way to the anthropological study of dance, then it must fit somewhere into the anthropological procedure. As Michaelis (1955) has noted, "the research and record film is an invaluable aid as an instrument of observation and description and as a permanent source of data that can be analyzed at leisure." Comparison is made possible both where a number of specialists view a single film and where one specialist views a number of films. In general terms, then, using film as a tool is in accord with traditional anthropological procedures.

More specifically, films of dance serve several purposes. First, film provides a record of a particular performance, rather than a record of a particular choreography in its "pure" state. And anthropologists are, in most cases, concerned with performance and stylistic variation, these being the essence of dance culture as distinct from choreography. Second, film is invaluable as stimulus material and for use in large-scale analysis of movement styles, as in Alan Lomax's Choreometrics Project. Third, film, or alternatively video tape, might profitably be used in studies of ethnochoreography or in cross-cultural studies of movement segmentation. Fourth, film is of inestimable value as a teaching aid to expose students to a variety of movement styles, to make them more "movement conscious," and to give them an opportunity to attempt notating

53

movement themselves. Last, film records continuity, thereby making it one of the best ways of letting us visualize dance, where so many elements are in motion together.

Film, like any other tool, also presents a variety of problems. Here I shall only touch briefly on two of the more significant ones.

The first of them—first in the sense that if it cannot be solved then we may ignore the others—is feasibility. This takes two forms: one is getting permission to film from the many levels of authority that may prove necessary, whether national, regional, state, or local. The other involves the actual physical difficulties of making a film: climatic conditions, sources of light and power, topography, and, of course, the human element. If one is just another interested spectator, one cannot expect one's fellow spectators not to jockey for a better view, refrain from spilling beer, walk or stand in front of the camera, or leap up excitedly causing one to record a panoramic, roller-coasterlike view of the crowd rather than the dance event. The alternative to filming an event in its natural setting is, of course, to arrange for a staged performance. This has its advantages as well as its disadvantages, and one simply has to weigh the merits case by case.

A second major problem with film is common to other areas of anthropological endeavor as well. This is the difficulty of shedding one's own cultural biases long enough to record others who are operating on the basis of different cultural biases. In filming, each time we start and stop the camera we are being selective, just as we are when we observe and describe an event. Cultures have preferences for styles and lengths of movement. If we are aware of them, we are less likely to impose our own preferences on what we shoot. Lomax gives the example of the West European bias for linear, punchy, abrupt, moderately long phrases, which cuts off the action inappropriately in cultures where the bias is for curved, flowing, longer movement phrases. His suggestion for lessening the effect of ethnocentrism is to observe phrase length, spatial geometry, placement of accents, and parts of the body most frequently used (Lomax, 1971a, 1971b). Thus we need to spend enough time in the society in which we will be filming to become familiar with its cultural preferences. While this will not necessarily allow us to film as would a native of that society, it is preferable to the kind of filming done by a naive observer.

In addition to the two kinds of techniques specific to the recording of dance data, we have a third technique, the significance of which goes beyond that of an aid or a tool. I refer here to field guides for the collection of dance information. I stress their importance not so much because they enable us to write down what we see about dance but rather because, if used correctly, they sensitize us beforehand to many of the things that may occur in the dance and the dance context.

There two kinds of field guides. Most of us concerned with dance research have developed our own guides for use with one or two specific dance cultures. But, as Kealiinohomoku so accurately observes (1974b:245-46), many who have had the frustration of coping with noncomparable data, with ethnographers who have witnessed important dance events but cannot describe them, and with anthropologists who "would gladly look at dance if only you could give us a guide or questionnaire," have gone on to develop guides for nondance specialists as well.

It is worthwhile quoting two of the rationales for these more universal guides. In 1952 Kurath published her Choreographic Questionnaire, saying of it, "At the moment we are not trying to convince sceptics but are merely placing a crude tool at the disposal of friends in other fields of research" (p. 55). Kealiinohomoku, in speaking of her guide, says that it

> was originally designed to orient the non-dance specialists who would be doing field work for some other purpose than the study of dance. This was coupled with the twin hopes that the field worker would have greater cognition of dance culture and would be able to obtain useful and accurate data to enrich his own studies, while providing a body of data for

ethnochoreologists who had not seen those dances. I hopefully envisioned a huge corpus of comparable data which would be available to ethnochoreologists for developing typologies and other comparative studies (1974b:246).

As Kealiinohomoku observes, and in accord with my own experience, the response on the part of the nondance specialists has been disappointing to say the least. The problem lies not with the guides so much as with the attitude toward them. People take them along to the field packed away in the bottom of a trunk alongside the 3 × 5 cards and the note slips. They generally do not give them a thought, much less a reading, until they are confronted with some event of which dance is an integral part. Then they dig them out and sit down to reconstruct the dance with the attitude that the guides will somehow provide a panacea. The result can only be disappointment. Anthropologists would not treat any of the other tools at their disposal in that manner. It would be inconceivable to go into the field without a clue as to how one's camera and tape recorder operate with the hope that one can push a button and as if by magic everything will set itself right and record all the data one wants. A closer analogy is the use of questionnaires. We would not administer one without having first read it to see if the questions are appropriate, or, in the case of a self-designed questionnaire, we would not administer it without doing a pretest. Dance data guides are tools like cameras, tape recorders, and questionnaires. Their effectiveness depends on the care with which they are used.

Many field guides exist but there are relatively few that are in any sense universal or usable cross-culturally. One of the best of them is Joann Kealiinohomoku's. It has three parts: 1) the Dance Data Guide, 2) the Material Traits Associated with Dance Check List, and 3) Dance Compendium Questions (in Comstock, 1974:250-60). The Dance Data Guide includes sections on writing shortcuts, identification of the dance background and purpose, identification of the dancers, dance structure and accompaniment, choreographic analysis, and movement analysis of

discrete body parts. If one were to study this guide before viewing dance and then were to record dance using all the detail
that the guide provides, one would have a record of dance
adequate for most purposes. One probably could not do a
structural analysis (in the sense in which Kaeppler and Martin
use the term) on the basis of this information, but the guide was
not designed for that purpose. The second part is what its name
implies: a checklist for the material traits associated with dance,
including such things as costumes, props, dance conditions,
musical accompaniment, and so forth. The third section, Dance
Compendium Questions, was designed so that "brief answers to
these questions provide the minimal data which field workers
should supply to archives and to dance ethnologists" (1974b:259).
Parts 1 and 2 taken together are more than adequate for the
needs of the nonspecialist, for the person observing dance for
the first time in the field, and probably for many of the purposes of the dance specialist. One of the most attractive features
of the guide is that it is written carefully so that it is meaningful
to the nonspecialist. When technical terms are used, they are
used precisely so that confusion is avoided. It is remarkably free
of jargon.

The two other "guides" I would like to discuss are not really
guides in the sense of having been designed to guide the researcher in the collection of data on the dance. They may,
however, be used to that purpose with great effect; they serve
too as excellent training devices for increasing movement
awareness and refining the ability to articulate this awareness. I
refer to the related systems of Effort-Shape and Choreometrics.

Even if one does not have the training to use Effort-Shape
notation, it is possible to employ aspects of Effort-Shape to
perceive and articulate basic qualities of any movement style.
The effectiveness of this use is aptly demonstrated by Bartenieff's comparison of the dances done by Yaqui Matachines
and Deer Dancers. The comparison is presented in the form of
a verbal description using Effort-Shape elements. First, Bar-

Table 1

Use of Effort-Shape Elements in a Verbal Comparison of Matachine and Deer Dancers

Style Feature	Matachinis	Deer Dancer
BODY ATTITUDE	upright, slightly concave knees slightly bent	straight torso leaning forward and upward into space, knee and hips bent at sharp angles
STANCE	predominantly narrow	narrow with some excursions into width
RELATION OF FOOT TO GROUND	bouncing off the ground	digging into the ground with high force and accelerations building up to explosive leaps
USE OF SPACE	linear, directional with frequent vague transitions	always linear and angular in transition
USE OF EFFORT Main Elements	strength, together with suddenness, rebounding into lightness	exaggerated strength, exaggerated suddenness, constantly recreated
ORGANIZATION OF EFFORT IN SEQUENCES	1) light arm gesture, holding twig: free flow strength developing into exaggerated suddenness being neutralized into light very bound flow	1) arm-hands using rattles: arm held straight forward-down or close to body flexed at sharp angle; rapid, small circular wrist shakes from the wrist with constantly recreated high strength-suddennesses, building up into bound vibratory shaking

Table 1 (Cont'd)

Style Feature	Matachinis	Deer Dancer
	2) step: free, swinging lower leg gesture becoming bound immediately followed by strong touching of ground ending in bound flow	2) step: digging step—small progression, digging into ground while sliding forward with high strength-suddennesses constantly recreated in a crescendo of bound flow, causing vibratory reverberations through whole leg and pelvis stalking step—exaggerated quick, free flow upbeat, moderately strong contact with floor, pause followed by head gesture quick, bound
INTENSITY OF INVOLVEMENT Gesture/Posture Predominance	alternate gesture/posture emergence	short gestural upbeat followed by long series of postural movement

From Comstock, 1974. Courtesy of Committee on Research in Dance

tenieff warns that a word description of an event "takes away the contextual framework; it may leave it with overcrowded enumerations of detail, without coherence, or end in disconnected ambivalence." Second, she emphasizes that this description does not constitute a full description in Effort-Shape terms, but rather "it enumerates a number of 'core' qualities, and they represent those features that, even in such a cursory observation as we were exposed to, stood out and could be 'memorized' as essential ingredients of this particular cultural style" (*in* Comstock 1974:185). The best of all possible worlds does not often exist for the recording of dance data. Given this, a system which even in the worst of field situations allows one to pick out and remember "core qualities" has advantages that cannot be overlooked. Additionally, a system that allows one to describe the relation of the foot to the ground in terms such as "bouncing off the ground" or "digging into the ground" rather than to have to choose between "leaping," "hopping," or "jumping," as in other systems, has much to recommend it to the nonspecialist.

Choreometrics is related to Effort-Shape in that it employs many concepts central to the latter system. This overlap was one of the design features of the Choreometrics project and shows the influence of Bartenieff, who is one of the collaborators. Data for the project are provided by films of dance and work activities around the world. The films are viewed and coded for either or both of these activities. The viewers record the film data on coding sheets which indicate the relative frequency or importance of particular features. A five- to seven-point rating scale which shows tendencies rather than actual frequencies is used. The coding sheet and the explanations of the abbreviations used in it could profitably be used by field researchers who are concerned with recording the gross structural features of a dance or dance complex. A less comprehensive set of features may also be used as a preliminary step, scoring the dance, for example, only in terms of three major features: body attitude, body parts most frequently articulated, and dimensionality of movement path. It must be emphasized, however, that neither the Choreometrics coding sheet nor the preliminary version of it will provide a complete description of a particular dance. They are designed to pick out gross features and they do it well. For some kinds of research this is perfectly adequate, and in some field situations it may be all that one can record.

Notation systems, film, and field guides are tools that allow one to carry out research more efficiently, and they are tools

Table 2
Choreometrics Coding Sheet 1, Sample

Date ___/___/___ Cord # _____ D _____ W _____ O _____ 5pt _____ 8pt _____ SL # _____

Culture _____ Gp # _____ . AR _____

Film Name _____ Source _____

Activity _____

	USE 1. Moving				2. Held					Syn 3. Moving					4. Held			
Tr	Ch	Be	Pl	Sh	Tr	Ch	Be	Pl	Sh	Tr	Ch	Be	Pl	Sh	Tr	Ch	Be	Pl	Sh
WL	UL	LL	Fo	To	WL	UL	LL	Fo	To	WL	UL	LL	Fo	To	WL	UL	LL	Fo	To
WA	UA	LA	Ha	Fiw	WA	UA	LA	Ha	Fiw	WA	UA	LA	Ha	Fiw	WA	UA	LA	Ha	Fiw
He	Fa	Mo	Ey	Fid	He	Fa	Mo	Ey	Fid	He	Fa	Mo	Ey	Fid	He	Fa	Mo	Ey	Fid
					5.	tot	M	/	F	6.	per	M	/	F					

7. Two Units	1	2	3	4	5	6	7
8. Type of Unit	R	M/a	V/	L-	U	U/L	T
9. Stance	N			W			VW
10. Relation to Vertical	V	|	C	)	/	⌐	P
11. Maintenance	D	C	A	H	H	P	R
12. Peripheral	1	2	3	4	5	6	7
13. Simultaneous	1	2	3	4	5	6	7
14. Successive	1	2	3	4	5	6	7
15. Central Impulse	1	2	3	4	5	6	7
16. Head Swing	1	2	3	4	5	6	7
17. Opposition	1	2	3	4	5	6	7
18. Disjoined	1	2	3	4	5	6	7
19. Multi-Systems	1	2	3	4	5	6	7
20. Vague Transition	1	2	3	4	5	6	7
21. Simple Reversal	1	2	3	4	5	6	7
22. Cyclic	1	2	3	4	5	6	7
23. Angular	1	2	3	4	5	6	7
24. Loop, 3-D	1	2	3	4	5	6	7
25. Curved	1	2	3	4	5	6	7
26. Linear	1	2	3	4	5	6	7
27. Indefinite Path	1	2	3	4	5	6	7
28. Small Range	1	2	3	4	5	6	7
29. Large Range	1	2	3	4	5	6	7
30. Fleeting	1	2	3	4	5	6	7
31. Strong Attack	1	2	3	4	5	6	7
32. Emphatic	1	2	3	4	5	6	7
33. Sustained	1	2	3	4	5	6	7
34. Strength	1	2	3	4	5	6	7
35. Acceleration	1	2	3	4	5	6	7
36. Slow-Fast	1	2	3	4	5	6	7
37. Fluidity	1	2	3	4	5	6	7
38. Jerky-Smooth	1	2	3	4	5	6	7
39. Light	1	2	3	4	5	6	7
40. Heavy	1	2	3	4	5	6	7
41. Variation	1	2	3	4	5	6	7
42. Tension (Control)	1	2	3	4	5	6	7
43. Focus (Precision)	1	2	3	4	5	6	7

Right-hand columns:

8s.	R	M/a	V/	L-	U	U/L	T
9s.	N			W			VW
10s.	V	|	C	)	/	⌐	P
11s.	D	C	A	H.	H	P	R
12s.	LA	LL	Ext-a-Ha				
13s.	T-A	T-L	T-H	T	A	L	
14s.	T-A	T-L	T-H	T	A	L	

| 17s. | T-L | T-L | T-H | T | A | L | |

Line #		BP.					
Dim	1	1-2		2	2-3	3	
Tr	1	2	3	4	5	6	7
Cir	1	2	3	4	5	6	7
Ch	1	2	3	4	5	6	7
Ra	1	2	3	4	5	6	7

Line #		BP.					
Dim	1	1-2		2	2-3		3
Tr	1	2	3	4	5	6	7
Cir	1	2	3	4	5	6	7
Ch	1	2	3	4	5	6	7
Ra	1	2	3	4	5	6	7

Line #		BP.					
Dim	1	1-2		2	2-3		3
Tr	1	2	3	4	5	6	7
Cir	1	2	3	4	5	6	7
Ch	1	2	3	4	5	6	7
Ra	1	2	3	4	5	6	7

Line #		BP.					
Dim	1	1-2		2	2-3		3
Cir	1	2	3	4	5	6	7
Tr	1	2	3	4	5	6	7
Ch	1	2	3	4	5	6	7
Ra	1	2	3	4	5	6	7

Line #		BP.					
Dim	1	1-2		2	2-3		3
Tr	1	2	3	4	5	6	7
Cir	1	2	3	4	5	6	7
Ch	1	2	3	4	5	6	7
Ra	1	2	3	4	5	6	7

From Comstock, 1974. Courtesy of Committee on Research in Dance

Table 3

Choreometrics: Coding Dance Styles for Body Attitude, Body Parts, and Dimensionality of Movement Path

Culture Region	Body Attitude 1-Unit	2-Units	Parts of the Body Most Frequently and Notably Articulated	Dimensionality of Movement Path 1-Dimensional Linear	2-Dimensional Curved	3-Dimensional Looped
Primitive Pacific	One		Whole leg, whole arm	Much		
Polynesia	Some	Much	Upper body, arm, leg differentiated		Much	Some
Africa	Some	Much	Head, chest-shoulders, arm, leg, differentiated	Some	Much	Much
Asia	Some	Some	Head-face, chest, pelvis, leg, arm, hand-fingers, differentiated	Some	Moderate	Much
Europe	One		Whole leg, whole arm; Moderate hand-finger, trunk, differentiated	Much	Moderate	Some
Amerindia	One		Whole leg, whole arm	Much	Some	

From Comstock, 1974. Courtesy of Committee on Research in Dance that increase one's sensitivity to the subject matter as well. Like all tools, they must be chosen with an eye to the particular situation and the particular research if they are to be effective.

❧ 4 ❧

STRUCTURE AND
FUNCTION

TWO PERSPECTIVES are basic to the anthropology of dance. They underlie all the research that has been done in the past, and they provide the foundations for two of the directions that the field will follow in the future. Structure views dance from the perspective of form, function from the perspective of context and contribution to context. In the past one could see a preference for structural studies in Europe and for functional studies in the United States. In Europe dance scholars with tested systems of notation at their disposal were collecting dance data and collecting it almost exclusively, whereas in the United States anthropologists with little or no dance background or collecting techniques gathered dance information along with data on every other aspect of culture. It is no surprise that the Europeans emphasized form and the Americans function. The anthropology of dance as a field has become more cosmopolitan now, and such clear-cut dividing lines can no longer be drawn.

People working in the field frequently express the desirability of marrying structure and function, of viewing all dance from both perspectives for the sake of completeness. That this is seldom done is not the result of perversity or myopia. It results, rather, from a combination of practicality and purpose. Structure or function is emphasized depending on the specific problem at hand. Structure and function represent perspectives which produce very different kinds of information, hence their utility in studies with a specific focus. Structural studies of dance traditionally have been concerned with producing "grammars" of dance styles. Functional studies, on the other hand, have concerned themselves with determining the contribution of dance to the continued well-being of a society or culture.

We will return to the utility of each perspective and to possible combinations of the two. For the moment, it would be well to see exactly what each perspective entails. "Structure" refers to the interrelationship between parts of a whole. In speaking of a structure, particularly in the early years of the twentieth century, people usually used an organic analogy. One of the more quoted analogies is the following by A.R. Radcliffe-Brown:

> An animal organism is an agglomeration of cells and interstitial fluids arranged in relation to one another not as an aggregate but as an integrated system of complex molecules. The system of relations by which these units are related is the organic structure. As the terms are here used the organism is not itself the structure; it is a collection of units [cells or molecules] arranged in a structure, i.e., in a set of relations; the organism *has* a structure. . . . The structure is thus to be defined as a set of relations between entities (1965:178-179).

It is important to distinguish between morphology and structure because, while they are often used interchangeably, they do not refer to the same class of things at all. Simply stated, morphology is concerned with form, whereas structure is concerned with the interrelationship of forms. Seen in this light, morphological analysis of dance is a necessary first step to a structural analysis.

65

In one of the first definitive structural analyses of dance, Martin and Pésovar (1961) made a number of statements which bear out this relationship of morphology to structure. Initially, they said that the organic construction of a dance can be revealed only by resolving the whole into its component parts. They therefore regarded as a prerequisite of any structural analysis the correct recognition and distinction of the parts and units of which a dance is composed. Here it is clear that they refer to the form, or morphology, of the dance. Applying a morphological analysis to Hungarian dance, they are able to distinguish parts that bear a hierarchical relationship to one another. The smallest indivisible unit of Hungarian dance, for example, is something that they call a kinetic element. This unit never occurs by itself but constitutes an organic part of the dance process, and it should be viewed as the result of artificial deduction. At this point an example of a kinetic element used by Martin and Pésovar should serve as clarification. The authors are discussing a motive that consists of three kinetic elements:

> 1. the right leg jumps sideways while the lower part of the left leg (the shank) swings backwards; 2. the left foot steps forward; 3. the right leg jumps backwards while the left leg swings forwards (1961:4).

They go on to state that, although kinetic elements cannot be divided into smaller independent movements, this does not mean that they cannot be analyzed and divided into phases:

> The third kinetic element of the above motive consists of the following phases: a) jump from the left foot, b) both legs in the air, c) right foot touches ground and d) bends a little while left leg swings forward and e) bends a little (1961:4).

The kinetic element functions in two ways: 1) several kinetic elements put together make up the minor units of dance, and 2) a kinetic element can be inserted between such units either linking them or forming them into major units. In the dance

66

structure, kinetic elements along with other similar units make up a category Martin and Pésovar call "parts." On the next level up we find "motives," which are the smallest organic units of the dance, that is, the smallest units whose rhythmic and kinetic patterns form a relatively closed and recurring structure. Motives exist in the consciousness of the dancer, can be remembered, and recur in the dance (1961:5). This is not true of kinetic elements. Motives fall into the category, "minor units." The succession, repetition, and fusion of the minor units and the parts make up the major units of the dance and through them the flow of the dance movements.

The creative aspect of the study by Martin and Pésovar lies in the structural analysis that grows out of the detailed morphological analysis they do. When they look at the *relations* between parts, they are concerned with such questions as the rules by which parts and units are combined and the resulting regularities in dance patterns. Once having determined the rules, they are concerned with the variations and the creative processes found in the dance. Hungarian dance, with its emphasis on improvisation, lends itself well to this type of inquiry.

Another concern they see developing out of this kind of study is that of eventually having enough structural analyses of Hungarian dance to enable them to construct a structural typology of Hungarian dance. They have devised a way of indicating the structure of dances that is midway between notation (Laban-Knust, in this case) and verbal description.

> If we want to gain a comprehensive picture of the structure of the individual dances and to compare the structural properties of the dance types, a schematic abstraction of the concrete forms is indispensable (1961:11).

To allow the reader to compare the notated score with the structural formula, I have included both notation and formula for a *Verbunk* dance (see figs. 7 and 8). For a complete explanation of the derivation and use of structural formulae, the best source is the original article by Martin and Pésovar (1961).

$$\mathbf{a}:\ 4\tfrac{2}{4}$$

$$A_1\left(\,a,a_v,\boxed{b}^{\,3}\boxed{c}^{\,2}\right) + A_2\left(a^2\,b\,b\,\boxed{c}^{\,1}\right) + A_3\left(a\,a,a,a\,\right) + A_4\left(a\,\boxed{b}^{\,2}\!.\,.\right)$$

7. Hungarian *Verbunk* dance written in Martin and Pésovar's structural formula. Compare with figure 8. *Used by permission of György Martin*

The structural analysis of Tongan dance done by Adrienne Kaeppler is more specifically based on a linguistic analogy. Kaeppler is also more explicitly concerned with "native categories" of movement than are Martin and Pésovar, but this may be because the latter are discussing a dance tradition in which they themselves are the "natives." Both the linguistic analogy and the native categories are set out in the following statement by Kaeppler:

> Just as a linguist working with a living language subjects a phonetic grid to phonemic analysis to obtain an inventory of the basic phonemes in a language, a dance ethnologist can subject an "etic" movement grid recorded in Labanotation to "emic" analysis in order to ascertain which movements have emic relevance and thereby obtain an inventory of basic dance movements comparable to the phonemes of a language (1967b:5-6).

Labanotation records every movement the body makes, thereby giving the researcher an "etic" inventory of movement. Not all of these movements are meaningful to dancers performing within their own tradition. Those that are significant make up an "emic" inventory of movement.

In the style of Martin and Pésovar, Kaeppler divides Tongan dance into units or levels of analysis. Her first two units correspond, I think, to Martin and Pésovar's kinetic element and motive. They are the kinemic level and the morphokinemic level. The first level refers to the forty-seven basic building blocks of Tongan dance, which are analogous to phonemes in language. The second level takes kinemes and builds them into

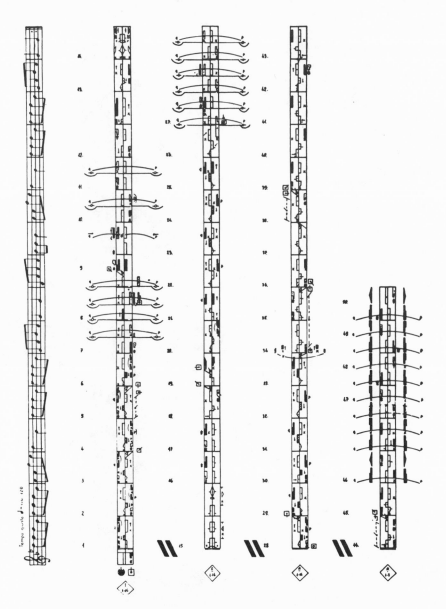

8. Hungarian *Verbunk* dance written in Laban-Knust notation. Compare with figure 7. *Used by permission of György Martin*

69

9. 10. 11. Hungarian recruiting dance. Nagyeced, Szabolcs—Szatmár County, 1955. *Courtesy of György Martin and the Photoarchive of the Institute of Musicology, Department of Folk Dance, Hungarian Academy of Sciences, Budapest*

recognized movements. Each of these movements is "the smallest unit that has meaning in the structure of the movement system" (1967b:103). These units, in turn, are combined in characteristic ways to build up units verbalized by Tongans as dance movements and called "motifs" by Kaeppler. The fourth and highest level of dance organization is the structure of whole dances. "A dance in Tonga can be described as a totality in which the structural elements have a standardized chronological order" (p. 4).

Just as Martin and Pésovar construct a structural typology of Hungarian dance, so does Kaeppler of Tongan dance. She tells us that, on the basis of her analysis and as recognized by the Tongans themselves, there are six genres of Tongan dance, each of which has a different combination of structural elements. She goes further, however, to include factors besides the form of the movement itself which affect the determination of genre.

> The differentiation of Tongan dance genres depends on three factors external to movement as well as movement itself. Type of music, the association of poetry, and the occasion of performance influence movement and must be taken into account when whole dances are considered. All four elements are also necessary to understand the role of the dance in Tongan society (p. 239).

Although Kaeppler does not do so in this particular work, she has certainly laid the foundation for a study of creativity in Tongan dance. Until one has a "grammar" of the dance, one does not know what the rules are and hence has no way of knowing how those rules are being bent or broken to incorporate change.

The study by Martin and Pésovar and the study by Kaeppler are undoubtedly the best examples of structural analyses of dance that exist in the published literature. It should in no way detract from their excellence to say that they are almost the only such studies. Structural analysis, properly done, is an ex-

71

tremely time-consuming kind of analysis at all stages in the anthropological process. Martin has been working with Hungarian dance as a scholar for the last twenty-five years, and has been an active dancer all his life. Kaeppler's original analysis was based on intensive fieldwork following a rigorous period of preparation. If we simply count the Labanotated scores, we begin to have some idea of the enormity of the task. As Kaeppler herself indicates, "analyzing dance with this method necessitates a knowledge of anthropology, linguistics, ethnomusicology, dance notation, and possession of moderate performing ability" (p. 309).

However much we may wish to view all dance forms and events from this perspective for the sake of completeness, in most cases it provides more information than is necessary for the particular problem. The costs must be weighed carefully against any possible benefits. Let me reiterate that the particular perspective or approach must be selected with a view to a particular problem. One may do a structural analysis of a dance type in order to produce a grammar of that type, but a grammer of the dance functions the same as a grammar of a language; it is a foundation upon which to build. It cannot really be considered as an end in itself, for then it is merely an exercise, a test of one's ability to observe and analyze. In this sense, it is also like descriptive ethnography, which is a necessary foundation but no more than that.

I see five potential areas of study for which structural analysis is a necessary foundation. Change is one of the areas, and here we can see the analogy between dance studies and anthropology in general. One of the rationales for viewing a culture or society as if it were frozen within a fixed time frame has been that, by so doing, we would have a picture of what that society or culture was like—that is, what its structure was—so that we could then document changes in the structure. In order to see change, we have to have an idea of what something was like before change occurred. If we have a grammar of the dance dated to a fixed time, then when change occurs we will be aware of it. This is particularly easy to see in a notated score if the changes are micro-level ones or in Martin and Pésovar's structural formulae if the changes are macro-level ones. It is simply a matter of putting the scores side by side and comparing them. We can also anticipate what kinds of changes are likely to occur, all other things being equal, because we know which areas are most susceptible to change.

Related to the subject of change in the dance is something we might call the survival potential of dances, and this in turn is related to the potential of dances to make the transition from local setting to theater. Dances with a greater number of what Kaeppler calls allomorphokines (dance movements on the meaning level that can be substituted for each other with no change of meaning) coupled with a less rigid sequential ordering of units probably adapt better to the stage than dances with fewer movements and greater rigidity. Because of its flexibility and hence potential for syncretic change, the former kinds of dances probably also survive longer in the local setting. To take two examples: Geoffrey Holder's choreography for the stage is effective because of the richness of movement in the Haitian tradition from which he is working. Haitian dance is characterized by both sharp and flowing movements, movements which are convulsive, as in trance dances, and movements which undulate, movements which are pantomimic and movements which are abstract. Also, because of the trance tradition, most dances are quite flexible in both temporal and spatial ordering. On the other hand, if we were to try to adapt Kwakiutl dance for the stage it would prove much more difficult. Kwakiutl dance is extremely repetitive because of the relatively small number of distinctive movements.

> All dances have fixed gestures and rhythms. In the Cannibal dance, the woman's War dance, and some others, there is a fixed fundamental gesture like a basso ostinato that is broken at intervals by special gestures of pantomimic character which are descriptive of the text of the song (*in* Boas, 1944:14-15).

Most Kwakiutl dances are solo dances for both men and women. All employ a very limited number of body parts: knee, trembling hands, head and arm in opposition. Women's movements are even more restricted than men's. Their arm movements, for example, consist entirely of the lower arm with the elbows kept tight against the side of the body. Men can, and do, use the entire arm. In many dances the emphasis is on mimicry, dances symbolizing killer whales, birds, and cannibals. The overall emphasis in all Kwakiutl dance is on keeping the dance movements in time with the complicated rhythms.

If we take the case of the Ballet Folklórico de Mexico and consider what is done to the basic folk material to make it theatrical, we will see the foregoing factors in operation. The basic steps of the Veracruz *huapangos* and *sones* and the Yaqui deer dance have not been altered significantly in the version that is presented to theater audiences. Both of these dance types are characterized by a variety of movements and a tolerance for improvisation; that is, the sequence of movements is not rigidly prescribed. Considerable liberty has been taken, however, with the dance context, story line, and spatial arrangement, especially as regards the deer dance (see Spicer in Comstock, ed., 1974). These dances are, however, intrinsically interesting in terms of movement, and therefore few, if any, changes are necessary in the form of the movements.

Other dance forms from other regions have much less potential for adaptation from local setting to theater. Consider the Isthmus Zapotec *sones*. In the Isthmus the basic step for women is a much modified waltz, reduced in scale both spatially and temporally, done with a modified *fandango* posture as a walk. In a good dancer the elbows do not leave the side, the skirt being raised alternating sides only so far as the lower arm can lift without moving the elbow. The men have a slightly more active repertoire of steps, including hops and *zapateados* (heel work but not as pronounced as in Spain). *Sones* are performed in open couples who move back and forth in semicircles, each partner moving in opposition to the other. The Ballet Folklórico has taken this basic material and exaggerated, activated, and reworked it. Now the waltz step has become a real *one*, two, three, with the first count featuring a bent knee and whole foot on the floor, and the second and third counts two small steps on the balls of the feet. The women hold their full skirts out at arm's length and balance lacquered half-gourds full of flowers and flags on their heads. Elaborate spatial arrangements characterize the Folklórico suite of Isthmus dances, from parallel lines crossing each other and reforming to sweeping circles by the men around the group of women, who are in two lines. Those elements of the prototype which in themselves would appeal to audiences have been retained, such as the extravagant, colorful costume and the proud, erect posture. Other elements have been exaggerated, such as the waltz and the *zapateados*. Still others are totally new, such as the floor pattern.

A third area that can be explored best by means of structural analysis is native categories of the dance. This area rose to importance within anthropology in the 1960s under the various names of ethnoscience and the new ethnography. As Kaeppler points out, her use of a linguistic analogy in doing a structural analysis of Tongan dance "by induction seeks to discover units and patternings valid in terms of a particular system" (1967:1). This use of linguistic analogy is first of all a way of arriving at the native conception of what constitutes dance in general, and, more specifically, it allows one to determine what are the building blocks of dances. One can make an analogy between hearing a foreign language for the first time and looking at an unfamiliar dance form for the first time. What are the significant units which make up that form? Even if there is a terminology for the particular form, it may not have a one-to-one correlation with the various significant units. Structural analysis tells us what units are significant to the "native speakers" of any particular dance type.

A fourth potentially profitable area of research involving structural analysis is one I call ethnochoreography, which deals primarily with native conceptions of movement segmentation. One of the first difficulties encountered in learning an unfamiliar dance style is the problem of unfamiliar phrase lengths. Assuming that it makes sense to those teaching one the dance to break it down at all (and often this kind of teaching does not have any place in the dance culture), what is a meaningful or comfortable size of movement for them may not correspond to one's own idea of a comfortable phrase. Until one can adjust to the unfamiliar length of phrase, the learning situation is difficult. What is important here is not the difficulty the phenomenon creates for someone who wants to learn dances but rather the import it may have for studies of cross-cultural variation in what is a comfortable segment of movement. From my own experience, it is clear to me that there is a great deal of variation between the phrases commonly used by members of the Ballet Folklórico, those used by Isthmus Zapotec women, and those that are comfortable for me on the basis of a classical ballet background. With structural analysis we can document these differences; with enough analyses we can say something about cross-cultural variation; and, finally, we may be able to see correlations between ethnochoreographic preferences and other aspects of culture. Robert Thompson has attempted to make similar kinds of correlations in his *African Art in Motion* (1974). He looks at preferences for certain kinds of patterns in visual arts and then sees if they are repeated in the performing arts, specifically music and dance.

A fifth avenue of research growing out of structural analyses, and perhaps the most important, is that which examines cultural values and norms regarding creativity. This, together with cultural values about aesthetics, will form the basis for Chapter 8.

We have considered the capacities of the perspective that views the form of dance, the structural. The other major perspective in the anthropology of dance deals with the function of dance. Within the field of anthropology, functionalism has appeared in various guises since the beginning of the twentieth century. They include functionalism based on biophysical needs of human beings and functionalism based on social needs, functionalism concerned with the individual and functionalism concerned with society, and functionalism, finally, that integrates all of the above aspects into a hierarchy of needs and controls. What all functionalist theories have in common is the assumption that all aspects of a society or culture contribute in some way to the functioning of that society or culture: "One . . . law of continued existence is that of a certain degree of functional consistency amongst the constituent parts of the social system" (Radcliffe-Brown, 1965:44). So we find anthropologists who value the functionalist approach classifying all aspects of society and culture, including the dance, in terms of their functional contributions. As we look now at the application of the functionalist approach to dance, we should do so with the awareness that functionalism is, ultimately, a way of classifying things. We can, for example, classify dances in terms of their different functions. Functional categories are useful for ordering data.

Perhaps Evans-Pritchard was reacting to the European collector tradition, which had dance as one of its foci, when he wrote that "dance is often viewed as an independent activity and described without reference to its contextual setting in native life" (1928:446). Certainly he did accurately describe much of what passed for dance scholarship at the beginning of the century in Europe. In looking at the dance literature today, however, we find at least as many studies that emphasize function and context rather than form and do so sometimes to the virtual exclusion of form. Evans-Prichard's own article on the Zande *gbere-buda* dance (1928) is a fine example of the contextual approach. He gives us detailed information about the organization of the dancers and supporters, the context of the event, and its social function without once mentioning the form of the dance itself. J. Clyde Mitchell is surely following this tradition in his article on the Kalela dance (1956) but does include a brief description of the dancing:

> The drums were hung on a pole in the centre of a fenced enclosure in the location and the dancers circulated round them in single file. The dance was made up of short shuffling steps ac-

complished by a slight inward swaying of the body. Periodically the leader of the band punctuated the drumming with sharp blasts on a football whistle, after which the dancers turned in unison towards the drums. During part of the dance the drums were silent while the dancers sang a song (1956:2).

A short description, yet at the same time it tells all that the reader needs to know about the dance.

American anthropologists also emphasized the functional aspects of dance. In *Coming of Age in Samoa* (1928), Margaret Mead stressed the important role that dance plays in Samoan life. In contrast to all other forms of social behavior in Samoa, the dance provides an outlet for the individual to demonstrate skill, excellence, and superiority. The dancer may innovate, flirt, show off, and be rewarded for it. It might be nice to know what Samoan dance looks like, but it is not necessary for Mead's purpose.

Studies that are primarily concerned with function but that, like Mitchell, include verbal descriptions of dance as well are those which constituted the two Boas seminars on the functions of dance in human society in 1944 and 1946. They are still among the best of the functional studies. The 1944 seminar included discussions of Kwakiutl dance by Franz Boas, Haitian dance by Harold Courlander, Balinese dance by Claire Holt and Gregory Bateson, and African dance by Geoffrey Gorer. The Holt and Bateson article, in fact, foreshadowed Lomax's choreometrics project when the authors posed the questions,

> What is the relationship between the movements characteristic of a given dance, and the typical gestures and postures in daily life of the very people who perform it? Gesture and posture in daily life are certainly expressive of a people's character, but how are their gestures and postures in a stylized, heightened, and intensified form, as they appear in the dance, related to their particular character? (Boas, 1944:55)

Writing when they did and where they did, Holt and Bateson were not much concerned with the relation between work gestures and dance gestures nor with positing an evolutionary dance sequence. Rather, they suggested that, by looking at dance, the anthropologist can find corroborative material for a people's cultural temperament:

> One field which still awaits exploration is the question of how far a dominant kinesthetic awareness of certain parts of the body is related to psychological factors. If posture and movement of an individual are closely interdependent with his psychological state, would not stylized posture and gesture in the dance of a people be relevant to a general psychological trend in their life? (ibid., 62-63)

We will return to the relationship between the dance and the psychological needs of people. First, however, let us look at some of the functional typologies that scholars have formulated for the dance. One of the first was posited by Gertrude Kurath in her summary article on the dance in 1949. Under a heading called "Universality of Purpose" she listed fourteen purposes or occasions where dance may serve a particular function: puberty initiation, courtship, friendship, weddings, occupations, vegetation, astronomical dances, hunting, animal mime, battle mime and *moriscas*, cure, death, estatic dance, and clown dances. The one disadvantage of using specific categories such as these is that one encounters the problem of comparability if one tries to apply them cross-culturally. Anthony Shay (1971) has attempted to resolve that difficulty by creating a typology of categories at a somewhat more general level. The following are his six categories: dance as a reflection and validation of social organization, dance as a vehicle of secular and religious ritual expression, dance as a social diversion or recreational activity, dance as a psychological outlet and release, dance as a reflection of aesthetic values or as an aesthetic activity in itself, and dance as a reflection of economic subsistence patterns, or an economic activity in itself.

In Shay's first category we could find somewhere a dance that reflects each aspect of social organization. These aspects would include groupings based on sex, age, kinship, friendship, ethnic background, and so on. Most societies have dances that are considered appropriate to particular ages and to each sex. Kealiinohomoku points out that, among the Hopi, women dance their entire lives but the particular dances they do change as they grow older. In other societies, Yugoslavia, for example, women cease dancing upon marriage. Still other societies require marriage and the responsibility it implies before people may participate in dance activity. Sex differences are frequently quite marked in the dance. The English Morris dancers, the Roumanian Călusari, and the Mexican Matachines are exclusively male, and the occasional female role is danced by a male in female attire. Among the Plains Indians of North America, only women were allowed to perform the scalp dances that celebrated the end of a successful raiding or war party. Female soloists performed the war dance among the Kwakiutl.

Divisions of society based on ties of kinship are also commemorated in the dance. The Bororo of South America are divided into two moieties (halves), each of which has its own dances and its own ritual occasions on which they are performed. In the winter ceremonials of the Kwakiutl Indians, novices are initiated by supernatural beings and upon their return perform a dance imitative of a particular being. The right to be initiated, however, is something that passes from father to son, daughter, or son-in-law.

Associations based on ties of friendship sometimes have dances that in some way symbolize that particular group of people. Ethnic groups frequently use dances symbolic of themselves to set their group off from surrounding groups. The Sardana dance, for example, became the symbol of the Catalan people in their rebellion against Spain (Spicer, 1971).

In the category of dance as a vehicle of secular and religious ritual expression, Shay includes such occasions as rites of passage (birth, coming of age, marriage, death) and religious ritual. He notes that there are three major types of dance associated with religious events: ecstatic or trance dances; masked dances; and solemn processionals.

One of the most universal functions of dance is to provide diversion or recreation. Occasions that are primarily social and recreational in nature usually stress the general participation of all who attend, with the additional stipulation that they enjoy themselves. This being the case, it is not surprising that the dances associated with these occasions are simple enough to be learned easily and performed without taxing either the mind or the body. Were they otherwise, they would defeat the recreational purpose. Dances requiring more technical skill, and therefore limited to specialists within the population, serve other functions.

We have already hinted that some dances serve the very important function of psychological release or outlet. Mead made the point that Samoan dance is one of the only areas of life where the individual is allowed self-expression and competition with others. Holt and Bateson discuss the fact that Balinese dance is characterized by sudden reverses of direction and stops that may serve to confuse the spirits, and, further, that the violent actions that typify trance dances stand in marked contrast to the everyday equanimity of the Balinese character. Among the Zapotec of Juchitán, the masked *mbioshoo* dancers cavort in the procession to the church, chasing children and kissing young girls who line the streets waiting for precisely that. In normal social interaction, propriety forbids any such display of affection. In our own rock dancing, extremely suggestive movements that would not be tolerated outside the dance context are quite common. We also have the dances that accompany rituals of reversal, when everything is turned on its head: the pauper becomes king; women become men; and license is the order of the day. Dance is one of the most effective vehicles for psychological release because its instrument is the human body. Feedback is instantaneous and catharsis immediate for both the dancer and the observer.

The fifth function of dance, in Shay's typology, is that of dance as an aesthetic activity. When raised in a Western tradition, we tend to reserve the term "aesthetic" for the high art forms of Western society. In terms of dance this limits dance as

81

an aesthetic activity to ballet and modern dance, although we have come far enough now to admit the classical forms of Japanese, Chinese, and Indian dance into that honored and select circle. Yet, dance is performed as an aesthetic activity and is hedged about by aesthetic judgments in any number of non-Western, nonindustrialized societies. A constraining factor is that of leisure and surplus. If a society wishes to have dance performed as an aesthetic activity, that is, where there is a dividing line between performers and spectators, then it must have a certain amount of leisure time in which to produce and enjoy dance performances. Since dances that are performed only by a selected group of persons are usually more technically demanding, the society must also produce a surplus so that it can afford to support performers who, at the very least, must take time away from their labors to learn and practice the necessary skills and then to perform.

These two conditions are met in many societies scattered around the world. Gorer, in speaking of the Wolof of Senegal, for example, makes the point that they recognize a category, *griots*, which connotes professionalism:

> There are the professional musicians and singers, called *griots*, who are the only people who are allowed to play the available musical instruments. . . . No music or dancing can take place without these people. The other group . . . is that of the courtesans . . . women who are renowned as much for wit as for complaisance and beauty. Their life is severely chaste, but they hold salons where the . . . best dancing is seen (Boas, 1944:26).

The Ashante have professional dancers attached to the king's court who perform for all state occasions. The Tongans, Balinese, and Hawaiians have a long tradition of spectator dance. Aesthetics as a topic in itself will be discussed in detail in Chapter 8. For now, it is enough to say that all peoples with a tradition of dance performance will also have a body of aesthetic values about the dance; that is, they make judgments about what is good and what is bad and why.

A more compact typology than Shay's and a more general one is that envisioned for the social sciences as a whole by Talcott Parsons (1951). He groups all possible functions into four categories: 1) pattern maintenance and tension management, which would include socialization and control over potentially disruptive elements, 2) adaptation, which refers to adjustments vis-à-vis the social and nonsocial environments, roles, and the division of labor, 3) goal attainment, or all of the goals of society, and 4) integration, which includes all the mechanisms like social control, power structure, etc. that bind the different elements in a society.

Frances Rust has analyzed the social dances of England by viewing the interrelationship of dance and society in a Parsonian framework. In her introduction she indicates that to be successful such an analysis has to meet the following requirements:

> (a) The basic pre-requisite that the item in question (the social dance) represents a standardized . . . item of social structure (to insure that it can legitimately be made the subject of functional analysis).
>
> (b) A detailed account of the item . . . and an analysis of its functions, in terms, for example, of the four problems enumerated above together with an account of the way it operates and interacts with other items, and contributes to the functioning of the whole social system.
>
> (c) Observation and analysis of any change in structure and function of the item . . . correlating such change in the larger social system of which it is a part (1969:3-4).

Few other published studies of the dance using Parsonian units of classification exist.

Assuming for the moment that we have decided to classify dances according to their functions and that, for this purpose, we may use any of the schemes I have outlined, the first problem we encounter is how to determine which function is predominant in situations where the dance has more than one function. A multiplicity of functions tends to be the rule rather than the exception. Functions may be regarded as either overt or covert and either manifest or latent. Overt and manifest functions refer to those uses which are acknowledged or put forth by the members of a society. Covert and latent functions are those meanings and uses which lie beneath the surface and which are ascribed by the analyst. For example, a dance performed by Tongans upon the occasion of graduation from a Catholic secondary school may be viewed overtly as a celebration dance or a dance in honor of the graduates. Its covert function is to demonstrate the unity and uniqueness of the Catholic minority as opposed to the Wesleyan majority. Likewise, a social dance in Western tradition may be overtly a time for recreation, while covertly it is a way of meeting and appraising prospective mates.

Any dance event, moreover, may have multiple functions at both levels. By interview and observation, we may rank these functions and thus determine some kind of priority. What one must keep constantly in mind, however, is that functions change over time and from one situation to the next. It may prove impossible and impractical to assign a particular dance to a particular functional category. For example, the identical dance, as far as form is concerned, may be performed at a Haitian religious ritual and as a tourist attraction. The function in the two situations is obviously different while the dance remains the same. Haitians would seem to be attempting to resolve or avoid any dissonance caused by this practice by referring to the dance by two different names ("religion" and "dance" respectively), thereby creating two different categories for the two situations. Donald Brown has documented a different solution to this problem of performing dances for tourists, that is, performing them out of their normal context. He describes the dance situation for the Taos Pueblo, who, when faced with the necessity of having dances that could be done for the uninitiated, borrowed dances from other Indian groups to use as "show" dances. This allowed them to retain the essen-.

tially sacred nature of their own dances. Faced with the same situation, the Haitians used the same dances but called them by different names. Yet a third response to a similar situation is the Tongan one, which took an old dance, modified its form, gave it a new name, and changed its function.

Just as structural analyses of dance forms contribute specific kinds of knowledge about dance, so do analyses of dance from the perspective of context and function. If functional analyses are to be meaningful, they must be conducted with a knowledge of their constraints and limitations. First, functional analysis is an ordering or classifying device with little or no explanatory power. Second, we must remember that any particular dance may have several functions, requiring us to determine primary and secondary functions. Related to that is the fact that functions may be either overt or hidden. Finally, functions are not always constant over time. We have seen examples of change in function for Tongan, Haitian, and Taos dance.

The study of dance has in the past devoted attention both to form and to function and context. Directions that dance study will take in the future will also be based on these two areas. Traditionally, attention to form characterized the approach of the dance scholar, while context seemed to be the heart of anthropological analysis. Dance scholars who are anthropologists as well utilize both approaches. Such unification of the field is both desirable and logically necessary.

PART TWO

Problems and Perspectives

❧ 5 ❧

THE HISTORICAL
PERSPECTIVE

THE EARLY period of dance history popularity was relatively brief, beginning in the first decade of the eighteenth century and culminating in mid-century. Called the Age of Enlightenment, the period was characterized by a propensity for the kind of scholarship that produces histories, among other things. As Palmer has noted: "There was a great demand also for dictionaries, encyclopaedias, and surveys of all fields of knowledge" (1963:291). It was also a period during which dance was an integral part of social life. Dancing was eminently respectable, especially in the French court, and much time and attention were invested in it. No one could hope to participate in court life without knowing at least something about the dance even if one lacked the natural grace and agility to be a skilled participant. So it is not surprising to find a number of multivolume histories of the dance. Two of the major histories of this period were written by Frenchmen (Bonnet, 1724, and Cahusac, 1754). The same period produced the work on dance notation of Rameau and Malpied. A third history of importance was written by the German Taubert in

1717. The intellectual climate in Germany at this time was propitious for compilations of this nature. Additionally, dance was a social activity of considerable importance. The tradition of dance suites was at least as well developed in Germany as it was in France. Still, that France led in matters of the dance is tacitly acknowledged in the fact that the largest section of Taubert's history is devoted to the theory and performance of French social dances.

After this first flurry of activity the practice of writing lengthy histories of dance languished until the beginning of the twentieth century. The next active period was ushered in by Khudekov's impressive four-volume work, *Istoria Tantsev* (1913), which was followed by histories written by a variety of nationalities and from a number of points of view. One theme underlies all of them, and it is different from the problems that concerned the earlier generation of dance historians: The emphasis on the distinction between folk dance and theater dance (Narodny, 1917, Bie, 1919, Kinney and Kinney, 1924, Hughes, 1933, Kirstein, 1935). At this stage there was little discussion, of an anthropological nature at least, of exactly what constituted the difference between folk and theater dance. Little was said either about their relationship. That this theme should have become popular when it did is very likely because both anthropologists and dance scholars had begun to go to the field for research. There, of necessity, they were exposed to dance forms often quite different from the classical forms preserved in written accounts by earlier scholars.

Another question of interest to early twentieth-century dance historians was that of origins. This had been, of course, one of the principal concerns of nineteenth-century anthropology. Since we have no physical evidence of what dance must have been like in its earliest forms, some have been tempted to assume that it resembled the dances of the most primitive living peoples. Some writers also suggest that dance of the nonhuman primates such as chimpanzees was a possible model for Stone Age dance (see Sachs, 1937).

90

A third theme characterizes the early twentieth-century collection of dance histories: a stress on psychological functions of dance, especially primitive dance. Dance historians were concerned with the ability of dance to induce cathartic experiences that stripped the individual of the suffocating trappings of civilization and confronted him with his essential nature. As we did with the other two themes, we can find parallel emphases to this theme in the society at large. Freud and Jung seem to have prompted movements aiming at psychological self-awareness and social consciousness. Adjectives such as "introverted," "extroverted," "ecstatic," "cathartic," "convulsive," and "mystical" abound in the dance histories of the period.

All of this bears a striking correspondence to what was happening in the world of theater dance. We see that the mystical, ecstatic tradition initiated by Ruth St. Denis and Ted Shawn drew from Hindu and American Indian dance. We find Isadora Duncan returning for inspiration to the ancient Greeks and arguing for a simple, joyful, emotion-producing and -releasing style of dance. Even that bastion of refined, constrained, and tradition-revering dance, the classical ballet, was caught up in a search for exotic sources, in a return to more natural forms, in an exploration of individual psyches, and in social commentary.

The Diaghilev Ballet Russes represents this breaking away from massed swans, fairy tales, enchanted princesses, and wicked sorcerers probably better than any other group. The exotic was represented by brilliant colors, lush costumes, and the Oriental postures and gestures in "Le Dieu Bleu," "Schéhérazade," and "Cléopatre"; social attitudes and commentary found expression in such ballets as "Le Pas d'Acier," a piece presenting the contrast between the life of a peasant and that of a factory worker, "Le Parade", another factory-oriented work described by the poet Guillaume Apollinaire as the "manifestation of a new spirit 'where reason demands that the arts march together with scientific and industrial progress' " (in Haskell, 1968:90), and "Les Biches," a subtle ballet by Nijinska expressing the twenties' attitude toward sex. There were also ballets on the theme of sports, like "Jeux" and "Le Train Bleu."

Perhaps most important of all in terms of anticipating the tenor of the times were the ballets that sought a return to the primitive and to nature. "Prélude à l'après-midi d'un faune" was premiered in the 1912 season of the Ballet Russes in Paris and, according to Stravinsky, was to show an archaic Greek bas-relief in profile (*in* Haskell, 1968:77). The public and critics were scandalized. Calmette, editor of "Le Figaro," refused to print the review of the ballet and instead wrote his own condemnation of it: "Those who talk of art or poetry in this connection are making fun of us—we were shown a vile and incontinent faun whose gestures revealed an erotic bestiality" (*in* Haskell, 1968:77). This particular work also brought the charge of Russian barbarism. The following year another scandal erupted at the premiere of "Le Sacre du Printemps," which Diaghilev and Nijinsky envisioned as being based on the primitive rites of Russian tribes. The first-night audience sat in great anticipation and excitement, and then the curtain rose:

> Not many minutes passed before a section of the audience began shouting in indignation; on which the rest retaliated with loud appeals for order. The hubbub soon became deafening; but the dancers went on, and so did the orchestra, though scarcely a note of the music could be heard. The shouting continued even during the change of scene, for which music was provided; and now actual fighting broke out among some of the spectators; yet even this did not deter Monteux from persisting with the performance. Diaghilev, who was with us on the stage, was extremely agitated; and so was Stravinsky. The dancers, on the other hand, were quite unmoved and even amused by this unprecedented commotion (Grigoriev, 1960:92).

Very few dance histories were produced during the twenty-year period between 1935 and 1955. The 1960s ushered in a brief return to the older type of historical studies, studies that had virtually no limits in terms of their spatial and temporal coverage. The one name that stands out during this period is that of Maurice Louis, who produced many articles and shorter works and then wrote *Le Folklore et la Danse* (1963), which includes one of the most extensive treatments of the popular dances of the Middle Ages that the literature knows. Still, Louis was writing about the same kinds of themes that were dominant in the preceding period: the themes of origin and evolution and the theme of the distinction between folk, popular, and theater dance. Taking the latter theme as his organizing principle, the Italian D'Aronco produced one of the few other broad historical studies of the period, *Storia della Danza Popolare e d'Arte* (1962). He also reintroduced the theme of sacred versus secular dance and, in a psychological vein reminiscent of the earlier period, spoke of Apollonian and Dionysian dance types.

The 1960s seem to have marked the end of this particular kind of historical coverage. No studies of import have been produced since. If we look again for parallels outside the study of dance itself, we find two factors that may offer explanation. A decline in popularity for massive histories in most fields of inquiry corresponds to an increase in number of problem-oriented studies or more narrowly focused studies. Additionally, the whole question of origins is no longer fashionable. If one is not concerned with tracing the origins of dance in general and documenting its progress through various stages, then there is little incentive to write dance histories that begin with Stone Age man and culminate in contempory dance styles.

Writing historical accounts of dance has by no means lost its fascination for scholars, nor has the number of such studies decreased. They are simply of another order. What we find now are accounts specific either to a dance type or to a time period or both. One of the best of the first type is the book by Marshall and Jean Stearns called *Jazz Dance* (1968), which traces the development of jazz dancing in the United States. The book is enhanced and set off from most histories because the authors not only rely on written sources but incorporate as well a wealth of material from interviews with jazz musicians and dancers.

Several of the recent studies have involved historical reconstruction of various genres of dance. Among the best are

93

Kurath and Martí's *Dances of Anahuac* (1964), an attempt to reconstruct the dances of the pre-Conquest civilizations of the Valley of Mexico, and Lawler's *The Dance in Ancient Greece* (1964), a similar effort. Both are significant, not so much for the specifics of what they tell us about the dance as for what they tell us about the *process* of reconstructing dance.

Kurath and Martí faced a somewhat more difficult situation than Lawler in that almost no documentary description of dance survived the Spanish conquest of Mexico. The accounts (one of which, by the Spanish priest Bernardo de Sahagún, is lengthy) that were written after the Conquest in an attempt to reconstruct the civilizations that had been destroyed cannot be relied on for total accuracy, since they were written by Spaniards, who were seeing what remained of the culture through foreign eyes. Kurath and Martí rely on a number of other sources of information including sculpture, painting, archaeological evidence for musical instruments, and comparison to present-day dances. Of course, the major obstacle is that the dance is an art that has both spatial and temporal qualities that are lost in any other format. In other words, the essence of dance is movement, which can only be captured imperfectly in sculpture or painting, however fine a representation may be revealed. What the two authors have done is to reconstruct a number of basic poses, postures, and gestures from what evidence exists. Then movement into these poses or postures is inferred, starting from a basic stance of neutrality or relaxation (see Fig. 12). Obviously, there are many ways to move from a neutral stance into any of the poses, but if one knows what kind of music accompanied the movement and if one has seen similar poses in contemporary Mexican dance, then one can narrow the number of possibilities considerably. We can never be certain of the resemblance between the reconstructed dance and the original but we can make some very educated guesses.

Lawler is fortunate in having more sources at her disposal. She relies on evidence from the following sources: literary, metrical (treatises on metrics and lines of verse to which dances

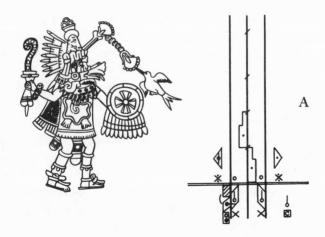

12. Reconstruction by Gertrude Kurath of pre-Cortesian dances. A. Impersonator of Quetzalcoatl-Ehécatl. The notation shows upright torso turned to right, arms flexed at shoulder level, sedate forward walk. Codex Magliabecchi. B. Impersonators of gods, in various stages of taking a forward step. The posture of fig. 12a is here expanded into a slow, majestic walk—"like gods," *teunenemi.* Codex Matritensis. *Used by permission of Gertrude Kurath and the Wenner-Gren Foundation for Anthropological Research*

were performed), musical, archeological, epigraphical (inscriptions dealing with the dance, lines on vases presented to dancers, and so on), linguistic (words and expressions in ancient Greek which connoted dance or related subjects), and anthropological (the use of comparative materials from the world study of dance and contemporary dances of Greece).

Both Kurath and Martí and Lawler deal not only with the form of the dance itself but also with the dance culture, including the role dance played in society, the participants, the status of dancers, and so on. For Kurath and Martí, one of the major concerns is the occasions on which dance was performed; in the case of the Aztec and Maya, they were primarily ritual rather than social occasions. The authors also discuss the role of dancer in these societies, who filled it, and the academies that trained dancers and musicians.

Lawler tells us that in the classic period of ancient Greece one of the more significant aspects of the dance was that everyone was expected to be able to dance creditably but not to the point of professionalism. Socrates was an outspoken advocate of universal dance training:

> He expresses high esteem for the dance, and recommends that it be taught more widely, for health, for complete and harmonious physical development, for beauty, for the ability to give pleasure to others, for 'reducing', for the acquisition of a good appetite, for the enjoyment of sound sleep (Lawler, 1964:125).

Aristotle echoed a number of other voices in his comments about professionalism: "No citizen should pursue these arts [music and dance] so far that he approaches professional status," and he went on to relegate all "professional activity in the fields of music and dance to slaves, freedmen, and foreigners" (Lawler, 1964:125-26). In this classical period, however, the professional dancers were highly trained and their dances were characterized by modesty and emphasis on the feet and gestures of the hands without exaggerated or lewd postures and gestures. By the Hellenistic and Greco-Roman periods in

Greece, the dance had definitely deteriorated, as had the rest of expressive culture. Lawler describes a visit by Apollonius of Tyana to Athens in the first century of the Christian era:

> Expecting to hear and see dignified and beautiful songs and dances from classical tragedy and comedy, he found the performers, in flamboyant costumes of yellow, purple, and scarlet, engaged in soft and effeminate dances to flute music, in which they impersonated Horae, Nymphs, and Bacchantes, and even winds and ships (p. 138).

Interestingly enough, the occasions on which dance degenerated into effeminate mime bore some kinship to a new genre of pantomimic dance which dominated Greece and Rome until the sixth century of the Christian era. Unlike the mime that offended Apollonius, the new genre generally portrayed themes from Greek tragedy or mythology. Indeed, as Lawler indicates, it probably saved much of Greek tragedy from extinction, since the latter had, for all intents and purposes, died out under the domination of imperial Rome. The best of the pantomimic dancers garnered enormous power by virtue of their talent and notoriety. This was in spite of the fact that they came from an inferior social position, because the admonition about professional dancers coming from the ranks of slaves, freedmen, and foreigners had not changed since Aristotle's dictum. Indicative of the dancers' power are the varied attitudes of the Roman emperors toward them. Some lionized them even to the extent of taking part in their dancing; others banished them or had them put to death; and one, Justinian, fell in love with one of the most skilled and notorious of them and married her, making her empress.

The phenomenon that the dancer occupies an anomalous social status and derives power from it is an extremely important one by no means limited to the pantomimic dancers of ancient Greece. A familiar example of hundreds that could be offered is that of Kchessinskaya. One of the reigning ballerinas of the imperial ballet of Moscow, she reigned as well as the

97

mistress of Tsar Nicholas II before he ascended the throne. Afterward she became the wife of Nicolas' cousin, the Grand Duke André. Unlike many of her friends and patrons, she remained a power after the Revolution. Lenin gave his first public speech from her balcony (Anderson, 1974:72). Although significant from the point of view of culture history, the documentation of the role of individual dancers in the societies of which they were a part is an almost totally unexplored area.

What is apparent from the kinds of historical studies of dance that have been produced in the last twenty years is that the focus is not so much on the dance form as it is on the dance as a part of particular cultures and societies. Again, one of the reasons for the change of focus must be the fact that we are no longer concerned with origins qua origins or in reconstructing the dance form from which all dances come. So, just as histories with specific focus in terms of dance style or time have replaced the massive compendia with an evolutionary slant, so have historical studies concerned with dance culture replaced those concerned with dance form.

Given that we are viewing dance as one aspect of human behavior, that is, from an anthropological perspective, then it follows that dance, like any other culture trait, can illuminate social and cultural history. Because it has not been used so frequently as other traits like religion, political institutions, and even music does not mean that it has less to contribute. There are situations where dance simply adds another piece to the puzzle of a particular historical analysis. However, there are other cases where dance is unique in what it can tell us about our topic of study either because information is carried best in a dance context or because the dance context is the only one in which that particular bit of information is to be found. Examples follow of dance used to illuminate history.

In a carefully documented piece of research Gretchen Schneider (1969) gives us an account of California gold miners during the mid-nineteenth century. We see gradual change in both the kinds of dance and the setting in which dance took place; *fandangos* and rough and ready polkas done in dance halls give way to waltzes, contra dances, and quadrilles performed in the context of formal balls to which one came by invitation only. Schneider sees this as a consequence of the gradual influx of women into mining camps that were initially populated only by men and visited by ladies of dubious background and repute.

Seeing changes in dance styles in much the same way—that is, as being responsive to changes in the social and cultural context—are two works that deal with British social dance. Richardson (1960), the more narrowly focused of the two works, talks about nineteenth-century social dance. This is the period that witnessed the demise of the minuet and the ascendancy of the waltz. The minuet and other figure dances presupposed a certain kind of social order with certain kinds of priorities. These were dances that, first, required more than average skill to perform, second, depended on access to dancing masters who knew the latest choreography, and third, required a sufficiently elevated social status that assured invitation to the balls where they were danced. The waltzes and country dances which superseded them were much more democratic in all three respects.

> Originally a mid-seventeenth century attempt to symbolize the chivalry of the Middle Ages and to revive the ideology of the Troubadors and Minnesingers, it (the minuet) had become toward the close of the eighteenth century a mirror of the artificial courtesies and the rich costumes seen at the Court of the Bourbons, out of touch with the romanticism which was already beginning to permeate the bourgeoisie of Europe, who for their dances were turning to folk and peasant song for inspiration (Richardson, 1960:41).

In the second, broader approach Frances Rust (1969) worked within a Parsonian paradigm to document the responsiveness of social dance to changes in British social history from the thirteenth century to the present.

13. Fancy ball at the California Exchange. From J.D. Borthwick, *Three Years in California*, 1857

Scottish dance from the Middle Ages to the present is documented in a work by Emmerson, and, like Richardson and Rust, Emmerson concerned himself with the relationship between dance and the social and cultural contexts:

> This book is primarily concerned with the character and place of Scottish dance life from the earliest times to the present. It is a synthesis of the cultural and social history of Scotland with dance as its centre (1972:1).

More than Richardson and Rust, Emmerson reconstructed many of the dances so that we know more precisely what the form was in addition to knowing contextual kinds of information. For this reason his history of Scottish dance is also an

100

excellent example of the process of historical reconstruction. Emmerson falls midway between Richardson and Rust, on the one hand, and Lawler and Kurath and Martí, on the other.

The pharmacologist Backman (1952), in his work on religious dances of the Middle Ages, not only documents the dances themselves and their contexts but provides us with an intriguing hypothesis about the impetus behind the medieval dance manias. He attributes the outbreaks of dance manias to ergot poisoning, and he substantiates his conclusion by setting out the etiology of this type of poisoning: the facts that ergot is a fungus that attacks rye and other grains after the grain has been subjected to a relatively long period of rainfall in the summer preceded by a severe winter, and that symptoms of ergot poisoning include the kinds of hysterical, contractive movements typical of the dance crazes. As further evidence, he presents his finding that there is a very high correlation between the years of unusually heavy rainfall and the years that saw outbreaks of dance mania.

Kaeppler's (1967a) analysis of the changes in the form and function of Tongan dance is another example of the added dimension that the study of dance can bring to culture history. This is due primarily to the importance of dance in Tongan society:

> Dance in Tonga has a pre-eminent social function; to pay allegiance to the socio-political system and to reflect and validate the systems of social distinctions and interpersonal relations (Kaeppler, 1967a:534).

Today the Tongan Islands have the status of a Protected State of Great Britain. Two factions split the population of the island and reflect both religious and political differences. One faction is composed of the descendents of the Tu'i Tonga line of kings, who are Catholic, and one is made up of the descendents and followers of the Tu'i Kanokupolu, who belong to the Free Wesleyan Church. Initially, and before European contact, the first faction held power. By the time the Europeans arrived, the second group had succeeded in overthrowing the first, establishing Wesleyanism as the state religion, and, since the Wesleyans had a proscription against dancing, banning dance.

Up to that point the dance situation had been relatively straightforward. There were two major dance forms corresponding to formal and informal occasions. The one for formal occasions was the *me'etu'upaki* (men's paddle dance), and the other was the *me'elaufola,* performed by both men and women—though not together—on informal occasions. The banning of dance created problems probably unanticipated by the new king. Since dance serves to validate the king's right to the throne by tracing genealogy and praising the king and his kin, and because the new king, by virtue of his recent coup, was not in the most secure position, he desperately needed a dance, his own dance, which would validate his right to be king, and maintain his position as acknowledged leader of his people. What to do? As the spiritual leader of the Wesleyan faction, he could not dance, but as the king of Tonga he had to dance. Covertly, the king collaborated with a well-known composer of dance and poetry and together they produced a dance, the *lakalaka,* which, although theoretically new, in actual fact derived from the old informal dance the *me'elaufola.* Having suborned the informal dance, they substituted for it the *tau'olunga.* This was supposedly an import from Samoa but in fact was an evolved form of an old Tongan dance. How did they avoid the censure of the Wesleyan Church and its missionaries? They said that the *lakalaka* was stimulated by the action songs used by missionaries in teaching children, reasoning correctly that any dance based on the same principles as the missionaries' songs would not be condemned by them.

The dance situation in Tonga has resolved itself so that today it has the following structure: the Catholics, still loyal to the Tu'i Tonga, dance the *me'etu'upaki* on special formal occasions symbolizing the Catholic Church, the *lakalaka* on formal state occasions where they show their allegiance to the acknowledged political head, and the *tau'olunga* on informal occasions.

102

The Wesleyan majority and followers of Tu'i Kanokupolu perform the *lakalaka* for state occasions and the *tau'olunga* for recreation.

This brief overview of Tongan dance should suffice to indicate that dance in Tonga plays a particularly important role. In a very real sense, the king cannot maintain his position as the acknowledged leader of his people without dance.

One of the articles that best illustrates the utility of dance history in adding to and clarifying anthropological concepts of social and cultural change is the comparative study of Balinese and Hawaiian dance by Kealiinohomoku. Her thesis is that if dance reflects culture, then any major culture change will bring about change in the dance and, further, that this change in the dance will either be consonant or dissonant.

> Change can bring new forms through syncretism if the new and the old are either supplementary or complementary. Without syncretism, disparate forms may arise, and old forms may become remnants known only by a few, unless and until viable reinterpretations occur to match changing functional needs (1973:2).

With these concepts in mind, she compares the fates of Balinese and Hawaiian dance through time.

Both Balinese and Hawaiian social organization exhibit stratification and stress ascribed status rather than achieved status. Balinese art forms have always been democratic in their organization and performance, however, whereas Hawaiian expressive behavior followed the pattern set by the rigid social stratification and relegated the refined performing arts to a select group of specialists. In Bali, dance and drama are culture-wide; they are essentially in the public domain; and finally, part of the fascination with a performance is the ability to rework and embellish the basic repertoire and have such innovations accepted. In Hawaii, on the other hand, both performance and spectatorship were limited to a select group, the symbolism was esoteric and equally limited to a small group,

103

and traditional aesthetic standards demanded adherence to convention and disallowed innovation.

When these two cultures were confronted with change in the society at large, their art forms were also affected but each responded quite differently to the challenge of change. Bali was characterized by syncretism or blending of elements, and selective adaptation, or selective acceptance of foreign elements, both in the wider social setting, as with their incorporation of Hinduism into traditional Balinese religion and rejection of Islam, and in their art forms. A large part of the explanation lies with a certain elasticity permitted by having the majority of the population as active participants and critics of the arts as well as valuing innovation. In the realm of the arts, Hawaii was unable to adapt in this manner, to blend the new with the old, and as a result the arts in their brittleness were much more susceptible to abrupt confrontation and loss. Only a small elite group was familiar with the dance tradition, and the tradition itself did not value innovation. This rigidity made the blend of old and new difficult, if not impossible.

The dance in Hawaii was functional only in the traditional social and religious organization. The historical view of the hula that Kealiinohomoku gives us bears out this conclusion, and we see the hula tradition coming full circle. At the time of Western contact in 1778, the hula was a dance form full of esoteric symbolism performed by specialists for the elite. Kamehameha's death in 1819 signaled the beginning of the disintegration of the traditional Hawaiian social system. One of the new co-regents, Ka'ahumanu, felt very strongly the need for change, particularly change in the tabus and mores surrounding women. Though she did not ban the hula outright, she did discourage it, and this had the effect of sending it underground, tainted by an aura of ill-repute. The coming of Christianity to Hawaii in the form of missionaries and churches merely added to the ill favor with which the hula was regarded. The hula experienced a reverse of fortune with the reign of King Kalakaua from 1874 to 1891, which ushered in a golden era of hula (Kealiinohomoku, 1973:10). The importance of tourism changed people's attitudes toward the hula once more. By the beginning of the twentieth century, the hula was a barely respectable tourist attraction. This attitude remained until the fifties and became more pronounced as the business potential of hula was realized. Sometime in the fifties, however, a movement was begun to restore many aspects of traditional Hawaiian culture, and one of them, of course, was the hula. It is impossible to revive the hula in its original form because too much has been irretrievably lost; the old social system that was its context no longer exists; few people are able to compose chants in the Hawaiian language, and so on. What one sees today is a "new" traditional dance (Kealiinohomoku, 1973:13). As for the reason for its restored popularity:

> The hula is becoming viable again because it has undergone a reinterpretation which can reflect the social organization of the contemporary society at large, a viable affective culture always does. Popular hula is no longer geared solely to the tourist, and serious hula is no longer an antiquarian relic (1974:15).

Because of its nature and the nature of the social situation, Hawaiian dance underwent radical changes in terms of its basic viability and finally has emerged with a different form and a different content, both the products of essentially Western scholarship.

In contrast to Hawaiian dance, Balinese dance has suffered fewer major discontinuities because it has evolved slowly by selectively adapting elements from contact cultures, by innovating in both form and content, and by syncretizing elements. Kealiinohomoku suggests that the difference between these two kinds of change may be that Balinese dance has experienced developmental syncretism whereas the hula has undergone acculturated reinterpretation (1973:18). This important distinction is part of the broader question of the relationship between dance and culture change.

105

Because dance is part of culture, it is subject to the same forces of change as any other aspect of culture. Response to change may occur in two areas.

Change may take place in the dance itself and this change may involve both the movements and the over-all structure of the dance—or, the form of the dance. Also, change can take place in the ways in which dance is used in society and in the reasons for dance performances—or, the function of dance (Kaeppler, 1967a:505).

In the example of Tongan dance, we can identify the change in form and the change in function. With regard to form, the older *me'elaufola* metamorphosed into the newer *lakalaka,* and the *tau'olunga* evolved from an older Tongan dance. With regard to change in function, the original function of the *me'elaufola* was as a recreational dance. When it became the *lakalaka,* it also became the dance used for formal occasions. The *tau'olunga,* on the other hand, remained a recreational dance.

We can see the same kinds of changes if we look at the dance situation Mitchell describes in his article on the *kalela* dance (1956). The predecessor of the *kalela* dance was a form known as the *mbeni* dance, which arose just after World War I in the northern Rhodesia area. The dancers wore mock military rank, and the dance itself was a parody of the local European community (1956:11). After the opening of the copper mines, which brought a great influx of Africans representing many previously separated tribes, a dance form known as *kalela* became popular. In its new form the dance has several recognizable characters based on European models—the king, the doctor, the nurse—while the rest of the group participate as drummers and dancers without any distinguishing characteristics. The raison d'etre of the *kalela* dance is to demarcate its members, all of the Bisa tribe, from all the other African tribes in the same area. The group does this in two ways: first, by singing songs that praise the Bisa and, second, by making fun of the other

106

tribes in still other songs. So, in the larger sense, the function remains the same: to mark the social boundaries between one group and another. The form, however, has changed as the significant categories that interact have changed. In the leisure setting, it is no longer the distinction between African and European that is the important one to mark but rather that between Africans of one tribe and Africans of another.

Dance may change either its form or its function or both, and change in these areas may occur independently. Whatever the magnitude of the change in any particular dance style, we may learn from it. Julian Steward, an American anthropologist interested specifically in studies of change, spoke about the use of dance material in these kinds of studies:

> The Bear Dance of the Uintah Ute no longer retains many of its older elements, for deculturation and restrictions imposed upon the dance by the Indian administration have altered both its purpose and nature. It remains, however, a matter of vital interest for every Ute and provides for the ethnologist materials for a study of culture change (Steward, 1931:263).

Applicable to the areas of both form and function are three basic kinds of change: 1) change that is gradual and that results from the imprecision introduced by oral transmission and learning by imitation, from slight differences from one performance to the next, and from deliberately introduced innovations; 2) change that results from selective adaptation of foreign elements and syncretism of the familiar and the strange; and 3) change that results from conscious revival, reworking, and reorientation of old forms.

The first kind of change is normal and inevitable given the passage of time. Dances vary, of course, in the rapidity with which they undergo change of this sort. Cultures that encourage individuality in dance style and creativity will probably experience more rapid changes in their dances than cultures that do not encourage these things. Likewise, cultures whose dances are part of rituals, the efficacy of which depends on the exactness with which they are performed each time, will have dances that change more slowly than those cultures whose dances are not bound up with such ritual.

The second and third kinds of change are associated with situations of culture contact. It has been common in the past, in speaking of change in general, to assume that change will occur more rapidly in the area of material culture, while the areas of values, ritual, and expressive behavior will be more resistant to change. It may be more useful to view whole cultures in terms of their greater or lesser ability to confront and incorporate change without doing violence to the basic pattern of culture. Kealiinohomoku has given us an excellent example of the different adaptation of two cultures to change. Bali is a case of a culture with an inherent flexibility that allows it to adapt selectively and, thus, to maintain its traditions over long periods basically intact and culturally coherent even though altered. Hawaii, in contrast, suffered discontinuities in its tradition of expressive behavior such that when it became important to return to the traditional forms it was necessary to revive them out of a past that no longer existed.

Two other examples will perhaps make the difference between the second and third kinds of change more clear. The Isthmus Zapotec provide a good example of the second kind of change in their culture in general and in their dance in particular. Since their move to the Isthmus from the more northerly stretches of what is now the state of Oaxaca, they have been constantly in contact with other peoples. It seems that on the one hand, their culture has always been flexible enough, to incorporate change without destroying its basic fiber, and that, on the other, Zapotec culture has always had the resources to resist innovations that might have irrevocably altered the Zapotec way of life. The traditional dance, *son,* is a rather recent development as far as we can tell from the historical material available. The first mention of it in its basic form dates from about mid-nineteenth century. Even then, it shows obvious foreign elements such as modifications of the waltz and the *fandango.* It changes slowly over the years although its basic pattern remains the same. Like Balinese dance, it is in the public domain and individual variation is expected and accepted. The *piezas,* dances derived from the larger national context, change even more rapidly, the waltz being popular at the turn of the century, then the *danzón, cumbia,* twist, rock and roll, until we arrive at today's Latin rhythms.

The example of the third kind of change comes from the Kiowa Apache, an American Indian group now living in Oklahoma. Removed from their homeland and surrounded by tribes with whom they were never in contact prior to removal, the Kiowa Apache gradually abandoned much traditional expressive behavior. When they danced, they danced primarily Plains dances, or those which can be defined as pan-Indian, rather than dances that could be identified specifically with the Kiowa Apache. There came a point, however, when enough people of the same mind agreed that they needed to be able to separate themselves from "Indians" in general and demonstrate their identity as Kiowa Apache. Like the Hawaiians who turned to revivals of traditional dances, the Kiowa Apache chose to revive some of the old tribal societies and dances. Again, as in the case of Hawaii, there were no members of the tribe who could reconstruct the dances as they were done originally because the tradition had lapsed into disuse. Eventually the Manatide society and ceremonies were revived and reinterpreted using a combination of the memories of older tribal members and the notes of anthropologists.

This third kind of change is becoming more and more common as individual ethnic identities are valued more and more. For many of these groups the emphasis on identity means reviving traditions that have long since disappeared, and so in a very real sense the revived traditions are "new" traditions, sometimes in form, sometimes in function, and sometimes in both. It appears that dance, music, and other arts occur regularly as important indicators of identity.

Related to change is something we might call the survival

109

potential of different kinds of dance. This is an important concern if we want to be able to anticipate the kinds of situations in which change is likely to occur. We can isolate eight characteristics that seem to give a dance survival potential.

1. Flexibility in the sense of serving more than one function.
2. Flexibility in the sense of not being tied exclusively to any one institution.
3. Flexibility in the sense of not being limited to a small elite either in terms of performance or observance.
4. A number of links with other aspects of culture.
5. A structure that allows for improvisation and modification.
6. Attributes that make it entertaining or potentially marketable.
7. Potential for marking identity in situations of contact.
8. The ability to change from being a recreational dance form to one for formal occasions and vice versa.

Much about change in dance form and culture is applicable to culture change in general. Systematic investigation of dance history or change over time should allow us to refine our concepts of change. In some cases, particularly in change of the third type, dance is a readily observable microcosm of what is happening in the larger social and cultural context. A case study of the change in American colonial dance is an example of the power of dance to illuminate happenings in the wider setting.

Case Study
AMERICAN COLONIAL DANCE[5]

Colonial America, particularly in the eighteenth century on the eve of the Revolution, has been characterized as a country and a people of paradox, exhibiting multiplicity, or unstable pluralism, and at the same time a uniformity, or national style

(Kammen, 1972:60). Different national backgrounds of immigrants, together with the American Indians already here, made up a very heterogeneous population. But, from the earliest years of the young colony, the environment and the ingredients were there that would brew a potent nationalism. The various immigrant customs and values were subjected to the test of a radically new environment and those that survived emerged irrevocably altered. The Dutch in New York, though they shared many things with their counterparts in the Old World, were simply not identical to them any longer. It was, indeed, a "new" York. In a sense, there was no going back save through the vehicles of nostalgia and sentiment. As the tensions inherent in being a young country subordinate to England mounted, it became more urgent to mold a more stable unity than that invoked by previous occasional appeal to national spirit:

> The settler's public rhetoric played incessantly on themes of union and unity. "Unity is the source of public happiness," Jonathan Mayhew insisted; "unity must subside and then it's plain what will follow," fumed the selectmen of Worcester, Massachusetts. "Our Ennemies never fail to take advantage of intestine divisions and confusion," wrote Cadwaller Colden in 1759, and the purpose of his exhortary plea was clear (Kammen, 1972:68).

As the tensions in colonial America grew, the national style became more and more clearly defined both on its own and by contrast to English ways. Americans had acquired yet one more identity.

The many identities were neither paradoxical nor problemmatical for those Americans who had cast their lot with the New World colonies. Which identity was paramount on any particular occasion—whether Scotch-Irish, inhabitant of Williamsburg, citizen of Virginia, or loyal American—depended upon specific contexts and pressures.

Paralleling the numerous identities, a number of dance traditions existed. Dancing was one of the most significant fea-

111

tures of life in the middle and southern colonies. As Stanard says for colonial Virginia: "There is abundant evidence that dancing was by far the most generally popular amusement in the colony" (1970:140). Fithian, tutor for the Carters of Nomini Hall in Virginia, also pays homage to the exalted position of dancing as he laments his lack of knowledge:

> After our return I was strongly solicited by the young gentlemen to go in and dance. I declined it, however, and went to my Room not without Wishes that it had been part of my Education to learn what I think is an innocent and an ornamental, and most clearly, in this province is a necessary qualification for a person to appear even decent in Company! (Fithian, 1943:43).

Burnaby, in his travels through the middle colonies in 1759 and 1760, remarks that the chief amusement for women of Pennsylvania was dancing in the winter and pleasure outings, of which dance formed a part, in the summer (1904:97).

It is clear that dancing was not limited to particular social classes or ethnic groups but, rather, was a pastime indulged in by everyone regardless of station. The kinds of dances popular and the occasions for dancing did, however, differ. Most of the eighteenth-century dance traditions can be placed in one or another of three categories: 1) regional dance styles, primarily ethnically determined, 2) elite dance traditions, primarily reflections of English and French dances, 3) national style dances demonstrating an American identity. Just as persons having several possible identities chose the one appropriate for the occasion, so did they display a number of dance styles, each appropriate to an identity.

It is in the category of regional dances that we are confronted by the number and variety of dances that reflected the heterogeneous nature of colonial America. The original inhabitants of the colonies, the Indians, danced as much or more than the later arrivals. The wealth of their dance tradition cannot ever be known, for our knowledge of it is restricted to the documentation by the occasional traveler or interested person.

Nicolas Cresswell, an English traveler in the colonies in the mid-eighteenth century, describes a dance among Indians in the Ohio valley in which he also took part.

> A fire was made which we danced round with little order, whooping and hallooing in a most frightful manner. . . . This is the most violent exercise to the adepts in the art I ever saw. No regular figure, but violent distortion of features, writhing and twisting the body in the most uncouth and antic postures imaginable. . . . The men have strings of Deer's hoofs tied round their ankles and knees, and gourds with shot or pebblestones in them in their hands which they continually rattle. The women have Morris bells or Thimbles with holes in the bottom and strung upon a leather thong tied round their ankles, knees and waists (Cresswell, 1928:109).

It is not at all surprising that an Englishman used to the regular figures of minuets and country dances should find Indian dances seemingly without pattern and strange in their violent exertions. Cresswell ranged far but one did not even have to leave the comforts of home to witness dances of Indians, as indicated in a letter from Trent Town, New Jersey, dated April 18, 1855:

> The ancient King of the Mohawks, (the same who was in England in Queen Anne's time) came down with some of his warriors this Winter to Philadelphia, and assured them of his friendship, though he own'd many of the young Mohawks were gone over to the Enemy; they were entertain'd at the Stadt-house, and made their Appearance also among the Ladies on Assembly Night, where they danced the Scalping Dance with all its Horrors, and almost terrified the Company out of their Wits (Balch, 1916:54).

In addition to joining in the dance of their fellow New Yorkers, the Dutch in New York also retained dances that they had done in their homeland. Evenings' entertainments always included dancing, and the final dance of the evening was always

"The Fire Dance," which, when possible, was danced around a chimney. Smith provides us with a lengthy description of this traditional closing dance:

> There was then a central chimney-stack . . . triangular in shape. On one side of it the great kitchen and its pantries extended through the entire width of the house, the fireplace occupying the center of the inner wall. On the other side of the chimney the space was divided into two large connecting rooms, each having a fireplace across one corner. . . . on this occasion there were sixteen couples in the kitchen and eight couples in each of the other rooms. The partners were arranged in rows opposite to each other in alternating vis-à-vis, so that when the gentleman of one couple faced his partner on the north, he of the next couple would face his partner on the south. The leading couple of each room advanced between the other dancers, bowing or courtesy-ing, and swinging alternately each other and every other gen-tleman and lady in turn as they went on between the files of dancers, with many stately steps and flourishes the while. The clasped right hands of the swinging couples were held as high as possible, the gentleman's left arm akimbo, and the lady's left hand holding her petticoats a little up, that her graceful steps and pretty ankles might the better be seen, until they reached the next room, where they became the "foot couple". The dance lasted until each of the thirty-two couples had led in the dancing round the chimney (Smith, 1966 [1900]:325-26).

As each lead couple came to the fireplace of the room farthest from the one in which they started, the partners recited some verses in Dutch and exchanged and drained glasses of punch, dancing all the while.

While English and French dances were being danced by both old and young in Tidewater and Piedmont, Virginia, the hardy Scotch-Irish and German settlers east of them in the Shenandoah Valley were maintaining dance traditions of their ancestors in the Old World. Even in households with strict ideas about worldly pleasures, the chief amusement for the young people was dancing three- and four-handed reels and jigs.

Another common dance went by the name of the "Irish trot." In all probability, the Irish trot mentioned in Kercheval's (1902) history of the valley was the New World manifestation of a named Irish step dance popular throughout the British Isles in the early eighteenth century. Step dancing, or dancing where rhythms are beaten out by the feet with the upper body unmoving, formed the basis for much Scottish and Irish dancing and characterized such dances as reels, jigs, and hornpipes. Dances out of the Scottish and Irish traditions also found their way to the musical stage in colonial America. John Durang, immortalized as the first American dancer, was famous for his rendition of a hornpipe in the theaters of Philadelphia in the 1780s and 1790s.

Blacks in the middle and southern colonies had their own dance traditions important for themselves but also for their influence on the dancing of the non-black population. Most owners allowed blacks to dance in the evenings and on Sundays, and a few owners encouraged dancing. Blacks often were granted permission to go to dances on neighboring plantations. Many owners viewed dancing as a healthful activity that promoted good tempers.

A variety of dances for different kinds of occasions characterized the black repertoire. Several types of dances were done by blacks in contexts where whites were absent or, if present, were limited to a few spectators. Animal imitation dances included the Buzzard Lope, Turkey Trot, Snake Hip, and Pigeon Wing. There existed also a genre that has been labeled "water dances." These, including such named dances as Set the Floor, Buck Dance, and Juba, all involved a test of skill in balancing a glass of water on the head while dancing. Juba and Buck dances appeared as well without the water balancing. Stamping, clapping, and patting were the hallmark of Juba dancing, for which is claimed an African origin by way of the West Indies. Emery also claims a long past for the Pigeon Wing and Buck Dance: "the Pigeon Wing and the Buck dance appear as authentic dances of the Negro on the plantation, much before they were

115

14. "The Sabbath among Slaves," From Henry Bibb, *Narrative of the Life and Adventures of Henry Bibb, An American Slave, courtesy of The Huntington Library, San Marino, California*

picked up for the minstrel shows and billed as the Buck and Wing" (1972:90). The Ring Dance, done in a circle by both men and women at the end of a night of celebration, was common throughout the slave-owning South. It was one of the few dances done by groups of people rather than by individuals or by couples.

Another dance that appeared everywhere was the jig. Much speculation about the origins, form, and impact on whites of this dance has been proffered. Burnaby describes dancing in Virginia: "Towards the close of an evening, when the company are pretty well tired with country dances, it is usual to dance jigs; a practice originally borrowed, I am informed, from the Negroes" (1904:57). Unfortunately, his subsequent description of the form of the jig gives the reader very little with which to verify or disprove his statement. Stanard takes Burnaby to task for his observation:

116

Burnaby thought that the jigs were borrowed from the negroes, but he was mistaken. The negroes had, and still have, grotesque dances of their own, but it is much more likely that they got their quaint jigs from the white people whose forefathers had danced them time out of mind in the old country (1970:141).

Basing her opinion on a description by Henry Ravenal of a jig performed at Christmas, Emery (1972:110) observes the striking similarity to the calenda dance of the West Indies described by St. Mery.

What is important to learn from this example of the jig is that there seemed to be a continual exchange of dances, dance steps, and dance forms between the black and white populations. This exchange led to changes in traditional dances of both blacks and whites through incorporation and synthesis. White influence on black dance is evident in dances attended exclusively by house servants (as opposed to field hands) which were composed of cotillions, English square dances, and other set or figure dances. These dances eventually found their way to celebrations of the field hands, where they were performed with a generous admixture of jig steps. The most faithful adoption of white dances occurred in the Quadroon balls of New Orleans:

> Because of the great emphasis on the "refinements" of the white race, it was only natural that the dances performed at the balls would be those of white society. Since anything Negroid or African was frowned upon by the gens de couleur, and since many of the quadroons had been educated in Paris, the dances were the same as those of a salon in France (Emery 1972:153).

Whites in both the South and North were exposed in a variety of ways to black dance. On the southern plantations, blacks provided the music for the balls of their masters and frequently provided dancing entertainment as well. That the children of their masters joined in the dancing of the blacks is documented by Philip Fithian. In two diary entries he indicates both this participation and his disapproval:

117

This evening the Negros collected themselves in the school-Room, & began to play the Fiddle and dance—I was in Mr. Randolph's Room; I went among them, Ben & Harry [Carter's sons] were of the company—Harry was dancing with his Coat off—I dispersed them however immediately (1943:82).

This evening, in the School-Room, which is below my Chamber, several Negroes & Ben & Harry are playing on a Banjo and dancing! (1943:83).

In urban Philadelphia many of the assemblies had for their musical accompaniment Johnson's band, who, from the descriptions, did somewhat more than simply play: "The music often was furnished by 'Johnson's band'—colored men—who made themselves rather obtrusive by joining in the measures with their voices. It was good dance music, however" (Young, 1898:77).

New York blacks congregated in Manhattan's Catherine Market, where, after selling their masters' products, they would gather and dance jigs and breakdowns for which bystanders would frequently pay them (Emery, 1972:140). Pinkster Day, held on Pentecost, was a popular holiday for blacks and one that provided an opportunity for dancing to the point of exhaustion. Most popular in upstate New York, Pinkster Day was also celebrated in New York City. One celebration in 1757 was documented by James Fenimore Cooper, who described it as "the great Saturnalia of New York blacks" (in Emery, 1972:141).

From the examples of American Indian, Dutch, Scotch-Irish, and black dance, it is clear that colonial America fostered a healthy and heterogeneous dance repertoire. In addition to these regional and ethnic dance traditions, there was a dance repertoire common to the elite whether they were scattered on plantations in the South or were residents of one of the northern urban centers such as New York and Philadelphia. In terms of social and economic backgrounds, rural Virginia and urban Philadelphia were quite distinct from each other. Philadelphia

15. Frontispiece from *Thompson's Compleat Collection of 200 Favourite Country Dances* (1777-82). *Used by permission of the John Carter Brown Library, Brown University*

reflected the interests of all social classes, from the ethnically diverse artisans to the middle-class commercial people who dominated politics to the upper class, who attempted successfully to establish British ways. Tidewater and Piedmont, Virginia, in contrast, had no great urban centers but rather were composed of a planter aristocracy, each of whom managed vast reaches of croplands and pastures from the family home. Ties were many and strong between the planter families, and their frequent visits were always occasions for balls. Just as their counterparts in Philadelphia did, Virginian elites looked to England for models of social life and culture.

English and French dances made their way to the New World in a number of ways. The New World elite made frequent trips to Europe and took advantage of their visits to learn the latest in fashion whether of dress or of dance. The sons and, infrequently, the daughters of these families were also sent to Europe to be educated. Part of their education included dancing. In the will of Charles Carter of "Cleve," Virginia, composed in 1764, Carter leaves instructions for his sons' education in England: "They shall continue at school to learn the languages, mathematics, philosophy, dancing, and fencing till they are well accomplished" (Stanard, 1972:292).

A third and perhaps more direct source of English and French choreographies took the form of dancing masters who emigrated to the colonies. They reasoned correctly that the competition would be less stiff and their talents more appreciated in a country with fewer purveyors of the amenities of gracious living. One of the earliest dancing schools in the colonies resulted from the combined talents of Charles and Mary Stagg, who had been indentured in 1715 to William Levingston of Williamsburg. "The Stagg couple had been bound to serve Levingston in the colony of Virginia in the 'Arts, Professions.' Levingston had been managing with the help of the Staggs a 'peripatetic' dancing school on New Kent and possibly in other nearby counties" (Land, 1948:360). We may safely describe the Staggs' repertoire as being European, and we may even more specifically describe the dances they were teaching as being those enumerated in Weaver's and Essex's translations of Feuillet's *Chorégraphie, ou l'Art de d'écrire la Danse*. These translations appeared in 1706 and 1710, respectively, and were among the effects listed as part of Charles Stagg's estate in 1736.

After the French Revolution a number of French aristocrats joined the ranks of dancing masters both in England and in the New World. One correspondent writing from Philadelphia noted that the "Virginia-Jig has given place to the *Cotillion* and the minuet-de-la-coeur" (Kelley, Jr., 1973:186). In fact, the minuet remained popular in America long after it had ceased to be danced in Europe.

The advertisements of dancing masters frequently reveal the kinds of dances they were prepared to teach. In 1738 Theodore Hackett advertised his services to the citizenry of Philadelphia, offering to "teach all sorts of English and French dances after the newest and politest manner practiced in London, Dublin, and Paris" (Young, 1898:39). A year earlier, in Williamsburg, one William Dering advertised that he could teach "all gentlemen's sons" to dance "in the newest French manner" (Stanard, 1970:143). The Chevalier de Peyronny offered his services to the people of Williamsburg in 1752, indicating his expertise in "the art of Fencing, Dancing, and the French Tongue" (ibid.:143).

Even though there were fewer dancing masters in America than on the Continent, the competition among them was still considerable, especially in the larger towns and cities. One gained prestige and therefore more pupils by being able to offer the latest in dance styles. One way of keeping up with the fashion was to acquire the notated choreographies routinely printed in England and France. Some dancing masters made trips back to Europe, while others received notated scores from correspondents. One of the annual celebrations for which dance scores were essential was the King's Birthnight Ball. This occasion was celebrated both in England and in the colonies. Rust describes the institution as it was in England:

> The court . . . continued to exert a great deal of influence on dancing in Georgian England, particularly through the institution known as the King's Birthnight Ball. A new dance was always composed for this occasion by the court dancing-master: it was printed in stenochoreographic notation [Rust refers here to the Feuillet system] for circulation to other dancing-masters and for sale to the public. Those people hoping to attend, or wishing to give the impression that they were going to attend, had to know the new dance (1969:59).

In addition to the King's Birthnight Ball, which was an annual event in the cities of the colonies and later became the President's Birthnight Ball, the elite dance tradition flourished in the urban centers through an institution known as the assembly. Balch, in his history of the Philadelphia assemblies, gives us the following definition: "The word 'Assembly' when used in a social way, meant in the eighteenth century that people who attended an Assembly gathered together in a social way upon a plane of equality" (1916:14). He goes on to docu-

121

ment dancing assemblies for Savannah, Washington, and New York. The early assemblies in Philadelphia, which first began in 1748, were governed by two sets of rules, one to define the times of the balls and the membership and the other to regulate the dancing. The former declared that the assembly would be held every Thursday night from January through May from 6 P.M. to midnight. The subscribers, fifty-nine gentlemen that first season, were to choose four from among their number to act as directors for the entire season. The directors had a number of duties: they furnished ladies with tickets for the assemblies, they furnished tickets for strangers, they received the tickets of admission every Thursday night, and they saw to the arrangement of the dancing and the card playing.

The directions for the management of the dances themselves are worth quoting in their entirety:

> 1. [Each set] to consist of ten couples. Such Ladies as come first to form the first Set, after which other Sets are to be composed that is in the order wherein they come to the Assembly.
> 2. Every Set of Ladies to draw for their Places. Only the first Ticket of each Set is to be reserved by the Directors to present to a Stranger if any, or any other Lady who is thereby entitled to lead up that set for the night.
> 3. The Director who has the composing of the Sets is whilst the Minuets are dancing, to couple those disposed for Country Dances and provide Partners for such Gentlemen Strangers who come in unprovided.
> 4. If there should be any odd Couples above a Set but not exceeding four Couples, they are to be distributed by the Directors among the compleat Sets, if above four Couples they are to be composed into a Set by taking some out of the other Sets. (Balch, 1916:41-42).

In his documentation of the Philadelphia assemblies from their inception in 1748, Balch allows us to follow changes in dance styles. We see in the beginning assemblies being opened by minuets, just as every state ball in Europe was opened during the eighteenth century. Balch recounts an amusing anecdote that documents the preeminent place of the minuet in 1749:

The Governor would have opened the Assembly with Mrs. _____but she refused him, I suppose because he had not been to visit her. After Mrs. _____refusal, two or three ladies out of modesty and from no manner of ill design excused themselves so that the Governor was put a little to his Shifts, when Mrs. Willing now Mrs. Mayoress in a most genteel manner put herself in his way and on the Governor seeing this instance of her good nature he jumped at the Occasion and they danced the first Minuet (1916:48).

From the rules governing the dances at the assemblies quoted above, it is clear that mid-eighteenth-century balls in the colonies revolved around minuets and country dances. In another example Young states that in the Philadelphia of the 1740s "the dances were almost wholly confined to the measured dignity of the grave minuet, although the English country dances were allowable" (1898:40). As the century progressed, travelers' accounts and new regulations for assemblies indicated that the favored dances now included quadrilles and cotillions as well as the perennial country dances. Both quadrilles and cotillions emerged as variants of the country dance in Europe. The quadrille was a square for eight dancers whose figures were composed of four or five of the most popular *contredanses.* In other words, when several *contredanses* were danced in succession by the same sets, the term quadrille was used (Richardson, 1960:58). The somewhat earlier variant, the cotillion, probably originated as a French peasant dance done by a number of couples dancing in a circle, which later became a square (ibid:48). Country dances were a little more flexible in that they could be expanded to accommodate more couples. One of the best known of the country dances and the only one that survived in England after the 1850s was Sir Roger de Coverley, known also as the Virginia Reel. This survived much longer in the United States, where it was the last dance at every ball until well after the Civil War (Stanard, 1970:141).

By the last half of the eighteenth century, there was more variety in the dances and the waltz was introduced, still a novelty and still notorious:

123

When a dancing-party was given there was always a supper. Cotillions and *contra-danses* were usual; sometimes a Virginia reel and a dance called the "Spanish dance." The galop was introduced about this time; the polka came later. Waltzing was frowned upon but the "fast" set, small as it was faced the opprobrium, while groups gathered around the waltzers as much to enjoy the wickedness as well as the novelty of the dance (Young, 1898:77).

Just as the waltz survived its initial reputation for wickedness in England and France, so did it survive and become fashionable in America. Kelley speaks of the German waltz being introduced and made popular at Oeller's hotel in Philadelphia in the 1790s (1973:171). Balch indicates the favored position of the waltz by 1839 in his discussion of the Bachelors's Ball given in that year, the "most splendid entertainment of the kind ever presented in this city" (1916:118), at which there "was much excellent dancing and waltzing to Johnson's brass band" (ibid:119). By 1849, Balch tells us, the polka was established in the assemblies of Philadelphia, again at an occasion that merited his highest praise: "It certainly was the handsomest ball ever given in this city. Breiter's Band was engaged and played admirably. He composed a new polka for the occasion" (1916:127-28).

Dances attended by the wealthy in Virginia and the southern colonies had a very different format from those in the urban centers, but with one exception the dances themselves were identical. In those colonies where plantation economy was the basis for everyone's livelihood the manor houses became the focus of all social activity as well. One indispensable feature of these homes was the ballroom and the adjoining supper room, which provided a place for refreshments to be served and for card games to be organized. Families took turns visiting one another and hosting elegant entertainments for each other's benefit. Holidays, christenings, and weddings were occasions that demanded celebration, but almost any occasion could be turned into a "company" event. The most important feature of any event was dancing, as is clear in the following passage from Stanard:

> There is abundant evidence that dancing was by far the most generally popular amusement in the colony [Virginia]. Wherever there was "company" there was dancing. Everybody danced. Girls and boys, men and women capered fantastically in jigs and reels, stepped forward and back and turned their partners in the picturesque country dances—later known as square dances, or quadrilles—tripped through the rollicking and immensely popular Sir Roger de Coverly . . . or courtsied low to each other in the rhythmic minuet (1970:140-41).

Earle agrees that the chief amusement for southern women was the ball, or country dance, and goes on to comment about the elegance of the balls even though they did begin in broad daylight (1962:209).

Some balls took place outside the usual round of visiting between families. In Virginia and Maryland men belonged to social clubs whose functions included balls that their wives, daughters, and friends attended. Balls to which prominent persons were invited were also given by the colonial governors.

Most sources agree about the dances that made up these balls. Fithian, already mentioned as the tutor for the Carter family of Nomini Hall, left a description of a ball that was given by Colonel Henry Lee on January 18, 1774: "About Seven the Ladies & Gentlemen begun to dance in the Ball Room—first Minuets one Round; Second Giggs; Third Reels; and last of All Country-Dances; tho' they struck several Marches occasionally" (1943:76). (Although an ardent observer of the social scene, Fithian was unable to dance a step himself, and I agree with Stanard that what he refers to as country dances with occasional marches were in all probability Sir Roger de Coverly.) In June of the same year Fithian described another ball: "the Company danced after candle-light a Minuet round, three Country

125

Dances, several Reels" (ibid:165). In his travels Burnaby mentions jigs and country dances, even giving us a description of the jig:

> These dances are without method or regularity; a gentleman and lady stand up, and dance about the room, one of them retiring, the other pursuing, then perhaps meeting, in an irregular fantastical manner. After some time, another lady gets up, and then the first lady must sit down, she being, as they term it, cut out; the second lady acts the same part which the first did, till somebody cuts her out. The gentlemen perform in the same manner (1904:57-58).

The sole difference in the kinds of dances performed at balls in the southern colonies and those given in Philadelphia and New York is the inclusion of the jig in the southern balls. Burnaby attributes it to black influence, while others see it as a result of the great numbers of Scotch-Irish who heavily influenced southern culture.

The jig did not, however, enjoy the paramount social position in the minds of those people who looked to England and France for models of social behavior as did the minuet, country dance, and all the variants of the country dance. It is not one of the dances mentioned on the programs of balls that celebrated the king's birthday, the coming to office of a new governor, or the rise to the throne of a new monarch. In a word, the jig was appropriate for occasions where one was at home in Virginia or Maryland celebrating events of purely local significance but was most inappropriate for those occasions where one wished to demonstrate one's loyalty and ties to England.

Another indication that the jig was not part of the Old World tradition that the wealthier segments of the population wished to emulate can be found in the description of dancing classes. The only dances mentioned as being part of the formal dance education of young ladies and gentlemen are the minuet and country dances. Those dancing masters who were thought to be knowledgeable about the fashionable dances of Europe were held in very high regard, and it was essential to have one's children educated by them. Mr. Christian, who held classes in the various manors of Virginia from the 1750s to the 1770s, was one of the highly regarded. He would go from one of the large homes to the other, being received at each as an honored, if somewhat eccentric, guest. The children of neighboring manors would come and spend several days being instructed together with the offspring of the host. Fithian describes one of Mr. Christian's visits to the Carter home, and confesses some surprise about the way in which the dancing master disciplines errant pupils:

> After Breakfast, we all retired into the Dancing-Room, & after the Scholars had their Lesson singly round Mr. Christian, very politely, requested me to step a "Minuet"; I excused myself however, but signified my peculiar pleasure in the Accuracy of their performance—There were several Minuets danced with great ease and propriety; after which the whole company Joined in country-dances. . . . The Dance continued til two, we dined at half after three—soon after Dinner we repaired to the Dancing-Room again; I observe in the course of the lessons that Mr. Christian is punctual and rigid in his discipline, so strict indeed that he struck two of the young Misses for a fault in the course of their performance, even in the presence of the Mother of one of them! And he rebuked one of the young Fellows so highly as to tell him he must alter his manner, which he had observed through the Course of the Dance, to be insolent, and wanton, or absent himself from the School (1943:44).

As far as the documents allow us to surmise, Mr. Christian was on no occasion chided for, or even questioned about, his disciplinary procedures. In view of this treatment of children of wealthy and influential men who together ran the colonies by someone who was after all "hired help," we must conclude that the knowledge he could impart was valued highly enough to allow an otherwise inexcusable disregard of the social hierarchy.

127

I have described the dance tradition of the elite as one which looked to the Old World for its models. The dances were Old World dances brought to the colonies in a variety of ways. Looking at the dances over time, we see colonial preferences changing along with tastes and, what is more, with very little time lag between them. On both sides of the Atlantic there is a progression from minuets and country dances to cotillions and quadrilles, and, finally, to waltzes ånd then polkas. Another indication of the importance of the Old World as a model of cultural ways and social behavior was the waning of British influence and the rise of French influence toward the end of the eighteenth century. Lamb, for example, described a ball given in New York in 1789 to celebrate the president's birthday:

> Two sets of cotillion dancers in complete military costumes, one in that of France and the other in the buff and blue of America, represented our alliance with that country. Four of the ladies wore blue ribbons round their heads with American flowers, and four were adorned with red ribbons and the flowers of France. Even the style of the dance was uniquely arranged to show the happy union between the two nations (1877: 342).

And we see the same process occurring in Philadelphia:

> Hardly had the British influence begun to wane than the French arrived in Philadelphia. The French minister, Gerard, entertained lavishly at his new residence, and twice a week it was the scene of balls, concerts and parties where the more influential Philadelphians got a chance to see the latest French fashions and hear the latest from Paris. Among the ladies "French hair dressers, milliners, and dancers are all the *tone*," one correspondent wrote; "The Virginia-Jig has given place to the Cotillion and minuet-de-la-coeur" (Kelley, Jr., 1973:186).

Oeller's hotel in Philadelphia was decorated in the French style and became a meeting place for those who considered themselves important in Philadelphian society and the more notable of the French émigrés, among them Talleyrand.

128

The acme of taste and style for this segment of young America was still Europe, but the favored leaders of fashion were no longer the English, whom we had defeated, but rather the French, fellow revolutionaries and allies.

We have thus far characterized the dances of colonial America in terms of two traditions: the first, or regional, which reflected the ethnic and regional heterogeneity, and the second, or elite, which was common throughout the colonies for those who looked to Europe for social and cultural models. We can, as well, isolate a third dance tradition. The national tradition seemed to have developed gradually and paralleled the growing sense of being a nation and the increasing discontent with being subordinate to the Old World. As the tensions in colonial America grew, the national style became more and more clearly defined until Americans had yet one more identity.

In that area where English influence traditionally had been strongest, the Atlantic seaboard, dissatisfaction with English models asserted itself as more and more wealthy families refused to send their children to England for their education into the ways of polite society. Virginia families now laughed at an English education saying that those who had gained one at great expense had only a stiff priggishness and lack of good manners to show for it (Morgan 1952:11). Such qualities as honesty, forthrightness, and democracy, formerly considered deplorable characteristics of an unformed society came to be seen as homegrown American virtues. European society generally interpreted these characteristics as naïve ignorance, roughness, and lack of a sense of social hierarchy.

This promoting of American ways versus English customs appears in the dance traditions as well as in other aspects of life. It was noted that the structure of dancing assemblies was much more democratic in the New World than in the Old. Places in the figure dances in seaboard assemblies, for example, were drawn by lot rather than awarded on the basis of one's social status, as was the case in Europe. The Marquis de Chastellux

129

comments on this in his account of a subscription ball in Philadelphia:

> A manager, or master of ceremonies . . . presents to the *danseurs* and the *danseuses,* folded billets which each contain a number, thus it is the fate which decides the partner which one is to have for the whole evening. All the dances are arranged beforehand, and the dancers are called each in turn (*in* Balch, 1916:88).

Every lady attending had a turn leading her set, and, if by some accident a lady was overlooked, it was the duty of the manager to rectify the error. The only favored positions at assemblies were accorded to unexpected guests and brides.

Perhaps the best way to summarize the tribute increasingly paid to the American virtues of simplicity and honesty is to quote from a letter written by General Anthony Wayne a short time after the defeat of the British at the battle of Monmouth:

> Tell those Philadelphia ladies who attend Howe's assemblies and levees . . . that the heavenly, sweet, pretty red-coats—the accomplished gentlemen of the Guards and Grenadiers,—have been humbled on the plains of Monmouth. The Knights of the Blended Roses and Burning Mount have resigned their laurels to rebel officers, who will lay them at the feet of those virtuous daughters of America, who cheerfully gave up ease and affluence in a city for liberty and peace of mind in a cottage (*in* Young, 1898:54-55).

Wayne refers here to the sympathy for the British cause displayed by many ladies of prominent Philadelphia families during the occupation of that city by General Howe. More specifically, he refers to one of the more outrageous instances of British sympathizing, the Meschianza. This was a fete given by some of the British officers in honor of their General Howe, who had been ordered to turn over his command to Clinton and return to England. Included in the spectacle were a grand regatta, a triumphal procession of the Knights of the Blended Roses and Burning Mountain with their ladies, a tournament, and a ball. The Knights were officers under Howe, and their ladies were "the fairest flowers of Philadelphia society" (Young, 1898:52).

Public sentiment affected the dance in a number of ways. Assemblies in the 1770s and 1780s selected their managers from among the most distinguished officers of the army. This position of honor previously had been the province of wealthy and respected civilians. In their names the dances done at assemblies and balls celebrated American patriotism and criticized the British. Some of the more popular included The Success of the Campaign, The Defeat of Burgoyne, Clinton's Retreat, and Stony Point. Earle comments on the fact that dances like these were used often as political statements:

> The dance, "A Successful Campaign", was the one selected by diplomatic Miss Peggy Champlin to open the ball, when she danced in Newport with General Washington to the piping of De Rochambeau and his fellow officers (1962:214).

The development and increasing popularity of a national style of dance did not mean that the regional and elite traditions were abandoned. Rather, all three traditions remained popular and viable. Which dance tradition was selected depended on the demands of the particular social context, so that by the end of the colonial period Americans actively supported three dance styles indicative of their multiple identities. The dance tradition used to symbolize the unity of the colonies and the existence of an American identity was part of the general repertoire throughout the colonies and was not specific to individual ethnic groups or social classes. At the same time, echoing the plural composition of American society, regional styles continued to be danced. Finally, the elite tradition continued, but with the substitution of French elements for the now unpopular English ones.

❦ 6 ❧

THE COMPARATIVE
METHOD

I N CHAPTER 2 we discussed the anthropological perspective and concluded that comparison was an essential part of doing anthropology. It is equally essential to the anthropological study of dance. The discussion of comparative method and how it has been and could be applied to dance is the focus of this chapter.

In the initial stages of observation we tend to see the unique aspects of all that is happening in the society around us. This is simply because we do not have enough information yet to fit all happenings into a larger scheme or pattern. At the same time, we are subject to the natural tendency to look for commonalities so that we can make the strange more familiar; so that we can say, "ritual X is not really so incomprehensible as it seems, for after all, it is very much like our own ritual Y."

This search for links between a foreign culture and one's own is accompanied by a tendency to look for similarities between events as a way of handling data that would be unwieldy if they were treated as unique occurrences. We may, for example, recognize the fact that each wedding is unique in a variety

132

of ways, but still we recognize aspects common to all weddings. In addition to allowing us to organize a great deal of information, this kind of categorizing enables us to anticipate events, one of the basic criteria of the adequacy of our description (Chapter 2).

Observation, description, and analysis are steps that must characterize the study of one culture or society, but, in order to achieve the goals of anthropology, they must be repeated in the comparative study of several cultures or societies. Edgerton and Langness state this quite clearly in their book on anthropological method:

> However well anthropologists may call attention to patterns of cultural behavior in one society, anthropology's ultimate goal is the understanding of man in all societies, a goal which can only be accomplished by making cross-cultural comparisons. Cross-cultural comparison involves a search for regularities in man's cultural behavior. But even more important, it is a search for wider theories of human behavior which bind these regularities together and provide an understanding of how and why cultures take the forms they do (1974:91).

Because we are looking at dance as an aspect of human behavior, we too share this wider goal. For us, it takes the form of a search for regularities in dance behavior. Beyond this, we seek as well the answers to how and why such regularities exist.

In 1954 Juana de Laban stated that the "folk dance field is virgin territory for comparative purposes" (1954:293). If no longer quite untouched, the comparative study of dance is certainly far behind almost any other area of dance research in terms of fruitful exploration. This same lag exists in the field of anthropology in general and for many of the same reasons. First, the tradition of field work is a relatively recent one. Only in the last eighty years have we been engaged in preparing careful descriptions of single societies based on firsthand research. The collection of dance data tends to lag even farther behind the collection of information on other aspects of

133

societies. In order to make cross-cultural comparisons, you must have comparable units to compare, something that has been conspicuously lacking in the area of dance. The reasons are several. Researchers have felt ill-equipped to deal with dance, and there have been relatively few of them working in the area of the anthropology of dance. Until quite recently they have also lacked adequate systems of recording dance data. Because of advances in methods and techniques and because of a recent growth of interest in the expressive aspects of human behavior, we should begin to see more and more detailed descriptions of single dance cultures or dance complexes. If we also proceed as anthropologists, then the appropriate next step is the comparison that will enable us to make statements about dance behavior in general.

Some excellent comparative work has already been done. The comparative studies that we now have fall into two categories. The first consists of works that compare the dance culture of two different societies or two different geographic areas. Into this category would fall such studies as Kealiinohomoku's comparison of Hopi and Polynesian dance (1967), Kurath's study of the dances of mid-Europe and Middle America (1956), Hall's essay on Noh, Kabuki, and Kathakali (1968), Royce's comparison of dance culture in four plural societies (1973), and Lomax's choreometrics project (1968).

The second category, less popular in terms of the number of studies, consists of research that compares the same dance genre as it occurs in different regions. Wolfram, for example, selects a genre that we may call "weapon dances" and traces its variations throughout Europe (1962). Bourguignon's work on trance dance would also qualify as this kind of comparative study (1968). In a narrowing of focus, Saldaña (1966) takes a character, "La Malinche," who appears in many dances of the southwestern United States and Mexico, and compares her manifestations in the different local traditions.

When we speak of persons who have done comparative research, we are once again confronted with the kind of problem that plagues any relatively new discipline. For the most part, the people doing the research are those who have had personal experience in more than one dance culture or with various manifestations of the same form and are working from their own data. It is difficult and perhaps not altogether useful to distinguish causes from effects in this regard. Although we know that there is a dearth of good descriptions of dance culture and form that in any way approach the quality required for careful comparison, it is not clear that, if the material were there, people would choose to use it. For a variety of reasons it is more comfortable to work with your own data. You know the circumstances under which the material was collected; you are more familiar with it than with other people's data; and you can be more certain that the units you are working with are comparable because you have probably anticipated this problem.

When you use material other than your own, you are immediately confronted with problems. Because you must put the various examples into some kind of comparative framework, you must rearrange the data at the very least, and usually you must condense it. In doing so, you run the risk of distorting the data by omitting a crucial element or by emphasizing something which in fact is relatively unimportant. There is no solution if you are working with very old material, but, if working with recent studies, you can corroborate your interpretation with the person who collected the original material. Such corroboration takes time and effort, again making it simpler to work from your own material.

If we are to take developments in the broader field of anthropology as models, then we must conclude that the way to progress for the study of dance lies not with comparative studies done by individuals, but rather with cooperative efforts that allow us to include many more dance cultures or forms in our comparisons. I do not mean to imply that smaller-scale comparative studies are somehow unimportant or represent some kind of early stage in the process of theory building. They provide one kind of perspective for which there is no substitute, for they can also consider detail rather than merely gross features, however necessary gross features on a large scale may be.

Perhaps the best example, certainly the best known, of comparison of the gross features of dance worldwide is the choreometrics project directed by Alan Lomax. We have mentioned choreometrics already in Chapter 3 with regard to methodology. For those readers interested in exploring the project extensively, I refer them to Lomax himself (1968) and two reviews of Lomax (Kealiinohomoku, 1974c, and Williams, 1974). Here I wish merely to speak about the comparative aspect of choreometrics.

Defining choreometrics as "the measure of dance, or dance as a measure of culture" (1968:223), and then crediting his earlier "cantometrics" project with serving as the inspiration for "choreometrics" Lomax arrives at the basic premise of the project:

> Choreometrics tests the proposition that dance is the most repetitious, redundant, and formally organized system of body communication present in a culture. The dance is composed of those gestures, postures, movements, and movement qualities most characteristic and most essential to the activity of everyday and thus crucial to cultural continuity (1968:224).

In addition to proposing this kind of one-to-one relationship between everyday movement and work gestures, on the one hand, and the kinds of movement found in the dance, on the other, Lomax also proposes an evolutionary ordering of dance cultures correlated with mode of subsistence. Using four major parameters—body attitude, type of transition, number of active body parts, and complexity of Effort-Shape—Lomax concludes that preagricultural societies (hunters and gatherers, pastoralists, and horticulturalists) have more simple movement profiles than agricultural societies. Preagriculturalsits tend to use one-unit body attitudes, employ simple reversal kinds of transitions, engage fewer body parts at any given moment, and have simple Effort-Shape profiles. In terms of comparative method, Lomax is looking for regularities in movement styles between groups of people with similar subsistence bases.

The procedure that Lomax follows is of more interest for us in terms of comparative method than his conclusions are. In the early stages of the project he and his specialist collaborators, Irmgard Bartenieff and Forrestine Paulay, devised a coding system (see Chapter 3, tables 1 and 2) which could be applied to films of dance and work activity. The system is intended to code cultural rather than personal styles of movement. This is an important point. Initially Bartenieff and Paulay were working with Laban's Effort-Shape system, but soon discovered that it was too fine an analytic tool for the kinds of gross patterns that they needed to code for large-scale cross-cultural comparison. Instead they developed a series of "motion qualities" similar to those envisioned by Birdwhistell (1957). Their importance for cross-cultural comparison is explained by Lomax as follows:

> These "motion qualities" run through all the behavior of a culture, controlling the way in which culture members handle energy as they go about their everyday lives. It is at this level that body style can be compared cross-culturally; profiles of such movement qualities can be handled by the similarity wave program in the same way as the song profiles to establish areas and regions of dance style (1968:230).

Bartenieff and Paulay then applied the coding system to over two hundred films of dance and everyday activities drawn from all the major world culture areas. These two hundred films represent forty-three movement traditions, or "profiles," which are then grouped into seven "stylistic regions" on the basis of common stylistic patterns. The regions are Amerindia, Australia, New Guinea, the Maritime Pacific, Africa, "Old High Culture" (which includes such cultures as Tadjik, Korean, Chinese, Japanese, Berber, and Uzbek), and Europe. (For a list of the forty-three cultures classified by style region, see Lomax, 1968:233.)

Lomax also derived even larger stylistic regions by selecting certain of the parameters of his choreometric system. For example, by distinguishing between movement "profiles" employing a "one-unit torso" and those with a "two-unit torso," Lomax divided the cultures of the world into two groups: the "one-units" of Amerindia and Eurasia, and the "two-units" of Black Africa, with extensions to India and Polynesia. Speaking of types of transitions, he finds that "simple reversals and other straight line transitions seem to prevail in the primitive world, whereas looping or curved use of space reaches its peak in East Asia" (1968:240).

Choreometrics is an ambitious attempt to say something about the worldwide distribution of movement styles. It goes farther than merely charting stylistic regions, for also it attempts to say why we find these regions where we do. As such, it qualifies as cross-cultural comparison on a large scale, and it is the only study of its kind. Curt Sachs also considered the distribution of movement styles and evolutionary sequences in his *World History of the Dance* published in 1933, but there exist major differences between the two studies in terms of technique and scope. Sachs worked from written sources and produced essentially impressionistic statements about styles. Lomax's coders work with film using a coding scheme designed specifically for dance and work movements. Furthermore, their judgments are subjected to appropriate statistical tests for reliability and inter-coder agreement.

If we consider the choreometrics project from the point of view of methodology, leaving hypotheses and propositions aside, we find that there are certain major flaws. The most serious of them, and the only one to concern us now, lies with the sample. Because of limitations of time and funding, Lomax relied on films already shot for the material to be coded. Thus, his sample is limited by the preferences and practices of amateur and commercial filmmakers. The fact that he is willing to use all kinds of films rather than only those one might call "ethnographic" or "professional" adds to the potential stock from which to choose. In preparing the study published in

1968, he and the coders worked with over two hundred films. But this was by no means a random sample or one that could be considered representative of all the world's cultures.

As Lomax himself points out, the areas remaining to be examined include Siberia, Central Asia, Southeast Asia, Indonesia, Latin America, and most of Europe, Africa, and South America (1968:235). Moreover, in the final selection of films, which resulted in the description of the forty-three movement traditions mentioned earlier, Lomax applied additional limiting criteria. For example, he omitted any films of the urban United States on the grounds that a dance style is hard to define for this area:

> Styles so frequently represent the evanescent fads flowing among subcultures. Instead we worked with movies of folk and primitive societies to find "pure" cases where movement style is more stable. Any observer, no matter how new to the field, is impressed by the extraordinary uniformity of movement style in any non-complex society (1968:230).

What effect this type of *a priori* selection may have had on the findings of the project, particularly where complexity of dance style is correlated with level of socioeconomic development, remains a matter for detailed examination (see Williams, 1974). For now, we might well be cautious in accepting global generalizations derived statistically from a sample of uncertain statistical adequacy.

Comparison, as I have indicated, may also focus on finer features of dance and dance culture. One of the best cross-cultural comparisons of dance of this kind is the study by Kealiinohomoku contrasting the dance cultures of Polynesia and the Hopi (1967). In her words, she has "tried to show how comparisons of the dance and gesture characteristics of two unlike cultures brings both cultures into clear focus. The uniqueness of each area is revealed through dance" (1967:356).

Kealiinohomoku initially notes some dance features that both Hopi and Polynesians share: dance is important and viable; dance is accompanied by song and uses gesture to rein-

139

force the song texts; locomotion is limited and leaps do not occur; and, finally, dances have supernatural powers. From there, she goes on to document the uniqueness of each area through contrasting gestural systems, performers, choreography, and performance style. With regard to gesture, for example, Kealiinohomoku states that "Polynesian gestures depict the legendary and empirical status quo rather than the sort of desired reality projected through Hopi gestures" (ibid.:347). We see a difference as well in the definition of performer. For the Hopi, men are the primary dance performers and for them it is a duty, an obligation to their tribe. A good Hopi performer is one who does not forget the dances, who does not seek individual praise, who has endurance, and who tries his best. In Polynesia both men and women dance, and whether or not someone will become a dancer depends on his or her interest, skill, and family tradition. Good performers are those who have individual style and who move well.

Kealiinohomoku concludes that Hopi dances are impersonal, conservative, and traditional. Dance for the Hopi serves to maintain tribal unity, placate the gods, and present tribal values. In contrast, Polynesian dances are personalized, less conservative, and encourage improvisation. Polynesian dance functions to commemorate events, entertain, increase mana, and propitiate the gods.

In the following case study of two American Indian pow-wow groups the focus is on the dances and dance structure of the powwows as well as on the social and political constitution of the two groups. Kealiinohomoku related dance culture of the Hopi and Polynesians to the larger cultural system. In my comparison of powwows, I shall relate the dance culture to levels of social and political identity.

Case Study
AMERICAN INDIAN POWWOW DANCE[6]

Traditionally, American Indian dance exhibited great variety and distinctive tribal patterns. Coexistent with the tribal dances were supra-tribal dance forms that today would be termed pan-Indian. These supra-tribal dances include the great dance complexes that swept the country during the latter half of the nineteenth and beginning of the twentieth centuries: the sun dance, the prophet/ghost dance, and the peyote dance of the Northwest and Plains areas; and the dream dance, which appeared in the East among the Potawatomi, Menominee, and Chippewa (Kurath in Leach, 1949:281). Dance complexes such as these were major components of revitalization movements that developed in response to the increasing threat to Indian identity.

Looking at American Indian dance today, we can still discern two tendencies, tribalism and pan-Indianism. They do not refer to the dance behaviors of two separate groups of people, but rather they are dance behaviors adopted for an appropriate occasion and they seem to have some relationship to local political interests. Each type of dance behavior is demonstrated and reinforced by two distinct mechanisms. Tribalism is strengthened by maintaining a distinction between public and private dancing and by reviving older dances and dance societies. Pan-Indianism is frequently demonstrated at pow-wows and at dancing contests. The dichotomy between public and private dances is aptly demonstrated by the dances of the Taos pueblo that Brown described in 1960. In Taos at that time dances were divided into those which could be performed only within the pueblo and those which were especially selected and choreographed for show purposes. This division was, in part, a response to the demands of tourism. Other pueblos had some dances which were not so sacred that they could not be viewed by outsiders, and these pueblos attracted tourists who enjoyed seeing Indian dances. As a response to the potential market, Taos acquired a whole category of non-sacred dances, some of them modifications of Taos dances, some new choreography, and some borrowings from Plains dances and those of neighboring groups. The existence of the two separate categories functions to maintain the integrity of such strictly tribal dances as Blue Lake and Kiva dances.

141

The second type of dance behavior that is tribal in nature is the revival of old tribal dances that have not been performed for many years. This has become an important phenomenon recently, with the revivals of the Ponca Heduska (Turley, 1966), the Oglala Sioux sun dance, and the Kiowa Apache Manatidie Society—the last discussed in Chapter 5 (Bittle, 1962). Again, this is a way of investing oneself with a more specific identity, as opposed to being an "Indian." As Indians have become more significant to the public, they seem to have separated themselves increasingly from the broader appellation, preferring instead to be identified as Indians of particular tribes.

Pan-Indianism, on the other hand, is a way of fostering and furthering a nationwide "Indian" identity. It too is adaptive in that it is invoked in situations where it is more advantageous for all Indians to act as a unified group. In terms of dance behavior, pan-Indianism is reinforced by dancing contests and powwows. Dancing contests frequently feature competition among adult males, who are judged on their skill in the war dance, a pan-Indian phenomenon, rather than on their knowledge of specific tribal dances (Slotkin, 1955). This not only encourages men to become skilled in a supra-tribal dance form, but it also serves to disseminate new steps or choreographies, making it difficult to maintain tribal dances in their "pure" form, if at all. The term "powwow" refers to a "social gathering where Indian traditional dancing and singing are featured" (Ablon, 1964:299). Like the dancing contests, powwows, particularly in the San Francisco Bay area, involve the coming together of Indians of many tribal affiliations, and they expose the participants and spectators to dance and song styles that are often pan-Indian in nature.

In the past, powwows have certainly served to promote pan-Indianism, and still do in many cases today. What is of interest is the fact that *tribal* dances and ceremonies are more and more frequently being revived and performed within the powwow context. In the comparison that follows we will be

142

concerned with the extent to which tribal dances, as opposed to pan-Indian dances, are represented and the relationship between this representation and the level of political activism among the participants of two different powwows.

For quite some time the several counties surrounding San Francisco Bay,[7] have attracted many Indians, who have voluntarily relocated there. The three large urban centers of San Francisco, Oakland, and San Jose offer diverse social and economic opportunities. Equally important is the fact that the American Indian is only one of many ethnic groups residing in the Bay area. In 1964, as reported by Ablon, Indian organizations and white agencies estimated that there were about ten thousand Indians in the San Francisco Bay area and that they represented some one hundred tribes. Oakland and San Francisco have within their respective city limits approximately four thousand Indians each, while San Jose accounts for the remaining two thousand. On the basis of Ablon's sample, the Navajo, Chippewa, and Sioux are probably the most numerous in the Bay area, as they have been in other relocation programs throughout the country. I have observed that these three groups are also the most numerous and active participants in the Oakland and San Francisco powwows. Other sources indicate that the San Jose powwow has a large Kiowa membership, but Kiowa are negligible in Oakland and San Francisco.

According to Ablon, in 1964 less than one sixth of the adult population participated, even passively, in the many Indian-sponsored activities in the Bay area. This figure rose somewhat in response to the Indian occupation of Alcatraz in November of 1969, but as of 1971 participation still remained quite low in proportion to the total population. Alcatraz seems to have had little effect on attendance at local powwows, which in 1970 was essentially the same as it had been in 1964. The audiences usually numbered between one hundred and two hundred people, and the active participants from twenty to fifty, including both drummers and dancers. This may indicate that powwows tend

143

to draw more people than other types of social gatherings.

Powwow activity in the Bay area is of two kinds: the regularly scheduled powwows and the powwows held to commemorate special events. In the first category are four powwows that are held on alternate weekends: the first Friday of each month is the powwow sponsored by the San Francisco American Indian Center; the second weekend is a dance at Cupertino; the third Saturday is the Oakland group's dance sponsored by the Intertribal Friendship house; the fourth powwow of each month is at San Jose. Various kinds of special events are celebrated by the second type of powwow. For example, two large powwows were held in celebration of the first anniversary of the Alcatraz occupation. Occasionally tribal groups will hold powwows for the arrival or departure of relatives or for birthdays. These are usually limited to the group and its friends. From time to time there are also benefits featuring Indian dances, songs, costumes, and sometimes displays of artwork. Because these are fund-raising affairs, it is desirable to have a large attendance and to attract both Indians and non-Indians.

It is useful to look at the social and political attributes of the Oakland powwow and the San Francisco powwow before turning to their dance structure. Looking first at the social makeup, we see that in terms of the tribal component the groups are quite similar. Chippewa play leading organizational roles in both. For 1969-70, the Bay area princess was a Chippewa, and she and her family attended both powwows regularly in traditional costume, dancing almost the entire evening. The Chippewa also sponsored many special ceremonies, such as giveaways and the dedication of a warrior drum. The remainder of the two groups is primarily Plains Indians, heavily represented by Sioux, and Southwest tribes. The same tribal concentrations are reflected in the drums.[8] At any given powwow, from two to four drums furnish music and song. The five drums most frequently in attendance at Bay area powwows were the Yellowsticks (Sioux), the Oklahoma drum, the Mockingbirds (Southwest, mainly Laguna pueblo), a Crow drum, and the warrior drum composed mainly of Chippewa.

144

Though similar in terms of tribal composition, the two powwows are unlike each other in terms of political awareness and activity. Broadly speaking, the San Francisco powwow is politically militant and the Oakland group is conservative. The former supported the occupation of Alcatraz. They raised money and supplies for the band of occupants and even sent members to the Island to teach Indian dances and songs. The latter, in contrast, ignored the occupation for the most part and occasionally condemned it. This does not mean that the group was totally inactive politically, but its activity seemed to be limited to producing individuals who were active in Indian affairs at the regional and national levels. The bulk of members took no part in politics except to affirm a generally conservative stance. In San Francisco there seems to be more awareness and activity by the membership at large, and more of a concern with an attempt to alter the fate of the American Indian in general.

The two groups also differ with regard to the age of members. The weekly dances given by the San Francisco group are attended by many people of both sexes in their teens and twenties. Although few come in costume or participate in the war dances or show dances, they do take part in the social dances that open and close the powwow. The Oakland powwow, in contrast, attracts few younger people. Its membership seems primarily to be middle-aged and older. Often in evidence are very young children, some of whom wear costumes and participate in the war dances.

Certain features of dance structure are shared by both powwows and they will be presented first. In the Bay area, powwows are held in rented halls generally in isolated or urban areas. There are restrictions that do not apply to powwows in outdoor settings; for example, no alcohol is served or sold, and the powwow comes to an end at midnight. Both of these restrictions are self-enforced so as to allay any fears on the part of people living near the halls whose complaints might lead to more severe regulations or even to the loss of a hall. Powwows are generally scheduled for 8:30 P.M. but rarely begin before 9:30. The beginning is signaled by one of the drums beginning

145

round dance songs. From one to five songs are sung before any dancers step onto the floor. The first dancers are usually women. This may be because the men need time to change into their elaborate costumes but probably it is because once the war dances begin the women have few opportunities to dance comfortably. With the exception of the Navajo and the Bay area princess, women seldom wear complete traditional costumes. Women of the Oakland powwow almost without exception wear or carry a shawl when they dance. This is not true of the San Francisco group, where a number of women can always be seen dancing without shawls.

The round dance as done on the West coast is the same as the one reported for Oklahoma. The dance circle moves in a clockwise direction facing the center drums, with the dancers stepping to the left on the accented first beat and closing the right foot to the left with a weight shift on the unaccented beat. A number of variations on this basic step are in the repertoire of most dancers: one features a sharp knee flex on the first beat; another has the basic step double time; yet another proceeds with the dancer facing in the line of direction (Powers, 1964:5). The dancers' arms are usually at their sides, but occasionally some participants will lock arms or even fold them on their chests. Both men and women join in the round dance, especially if it occurs again later in the powwow. It affords noncostumed young people and older males an opportunity to dance which is denied them in the war dances that comprise the bulk of the powwow repertoire.

The opening round dance continues until the costumed dancers begin to appear. At this point the drums change to war dance songs. Like many dances, the war dances have lost their original function and have become primarily show pieces (Kurath, 1949:1166). Both fast and slow war dances are performed, the fast being reserved for the last half of the powwow. The direction of the circle is clockwise, with women and men mingling in the same circle. This is in keeping with the Oklahoma custom in contrast to the northern Plains style. The

146

women generally do conservative steps using the full foot rather than the toe-heel or toe-flat stepping characteristic of men's war dances. I have seen exceptions to this apparent conservatism on the part of women but rarely and then only during the fast war dances at the San Francisco powwow. In both pow-wows most men elaborate on the straight war dance style during fast war dances, with the addition of fast turns on one foot, crossovers of the legs and feet, sudden drops into crouching positions, and rapid weight shifts that create a rocking motion. The Sioux are an exception. They rarely add these embellishments, only occasionally using the weight shifts. The Sioux typically tend toward tribal integrity in their dancing.

Two dances related to the war dances also appear in the powwow repertoire, and both are performed at the end of the dancing. One is the "trot" dance, characterized by the dancer's legs moving alternately, stepping flat-footed on each drumbeat. This dance is performed only when the singers and dancers are in high spirits and the powwow is moving quickly and well (Turley, 1966:3). The other dance, usually occurring at the very end, is the "stop" war dance song, reported by Turley to be a northern Plains phenomenon. It is a song designed to trick the dancer into missing the ending. Stopping on precisely the last beat is one of the most important criteria for being a good war dancer, and, in fact, failure to do so automatically eliminates a dancer from a contest (Slotkin, 1955). In the "stop" version of the war dance song, the drum sings three phrases of the chorus and then on the repeat chorus the stop is made after the repetition of phrase two instead of going on to conclude with phrase three. A good dancer should be able to recognize these "stop" songs and finish on the last drumbeat as he normally does. If a dancer is tricked, however, it is a source of much amusement and good-natured teasing.

Sometimes, rather than concluding with a war dance, the powwow will use the rabbit dance instead. This happens more frequently in San Francisco than in Oakland. Whether or not the rabbit dance is performed depends on the number of couples who are willing to take part rather than on any formal structure. In Oakland this dance is announced both as the rabbit dance, which is Sioux and northern Plains usage, and as the two-step, which is Oklahoma terminology. The dance is done by couples in a modified skater's position who travel in a clockwise circle. The basic step pattern takes six counts and begins with the left foot stepping forward (1), the right leg closing to the left (2), with a weight shift, a repeat of this phrase (3 and 4), then a step back with the left (5), and another step back with the right (6) (Powers, 1965:6).

Modifications of this basic dance structure in Bay area pow-wows occur whenever occasional special dances such as blanket dances, giveaways, and individual versions of specialties like the hoop dance are added. One ceremony, the dedication of a new warrior drum sponsored by the Oakland Chippewa in the fall of 1970, is worthy of closer examination because, while it incorporated both tribal and pan-Indian elements, it was consciously tribal in spirit and purpose. It is significant that this revival of an old tribal ceremony should have been performed at the politically conservative and tribally inclined Oakland powwow.

The warrior drum arrived covered by a blanket at 9:50 P.M. and was placed at the head of the line of three other drums, all in the center of the hall. The dedication ceremony itself began at 10:30 with the solo singing of the Sky City song with no drum accompaniment. In full tribal regalia the Chippewa directing the ceremony then turned to a member of the Oklahoma drum and asked him to say a prayer in his own language requesting the blessing of the Great Spirit. The man demurred, and finally a member of the Mockingbird drum, a man from Laguna pueblo, was selected and he gave a rather long invocation. Following this, the Peace Pipe ceremony began, performed by a second Chippewa (dressed like the first but with the addition of a war bonnet) to an "appropriate" song from the Oakland drum. I say "appropriate" because it was not the song originally companying this particular ceremony. With the pipe he made two counter-clockwise circuits of the drum, using the toe-flat step of the straight war dance. This was the first and only time I ever observed a counter-clockwise circle at either powwow. Of still greater interest is the fact that it is the reverse of the aboriginal circle direction for the Chippewa in general, and, more specifically, of the Chippewa circle during drum presentation ceremonies (Densmore, 1913:168). I can offer no explanation for this reversal, but it caused no concern among either participants or spectators.

The Chippewa continued with a third circuit, this time stopping at each of the cardinal points to raise the pipe skyward with one end to his mouth, and then to lower it toward the drum. During this selection the audience was requested to stand. Singers were then selected for the new drum. In what perhaps may be described as a spirit of ecumenicism, the six men chosen represented six different tribes: Nez Percé, Navajo, Kiowa, Chippewa, Crow, and Comanche. With the men seated around the drum, the pipe was passed from singer to singer in a counter-clockwise direction and each was given a new drumstick. The blanket covering the drum was removed and folded up while a prayer was read in Chippewa. The new drum sang a song, and then the dancers were invited to join in a war dance.

The old and the new, tribal and pan-Indian, appear all through this ceremony. Tribal elements include the prayers in the various Indian languages, the use of the peace pipe in drum-presentation ritual (which has precedents in Chippewa custom), and the wearing of Chippewa dress. Pan-Indian elements include the use of the Oklahoma drum for the pipe ceremony, the pan-Plains dance step, the varied tribal composition of the new drum, the absence of traditional dress for the singers, and the southern Plains war-dance song. For the powwow participants and spectators, however, this was a Chippewa ceremony, not a pan-Indian one. The "authenticity" of each element matters little in terms of the overall purpose. Indeed, it would be difficult to say whether the Chippewa drum ceremony as Densmore recorded it at the beginning of this century was

149

the "authentic" version. As we have already noted in speaking about change, people can quite easily accommodate changes in both the form and the function of dance. It is possible to use a totally syncretized dance form to symbolize a traditional identity. The important point for this study is that such tribal-derived and tribal-oriented ceremonies happened with relative frequency in the Oakland powwow and were rare in San Francisco.

The powwow repertoire in the Bay area includes two types of dance forms: those pan-Indian social dances that are easily learned, do not require costumes, and encourage the participation of everyone—male, female, young, old, and even non-Indian—and those dances, often tribal-specific, that demand knowledge and skill, require lavish costumes, and frequently are limited to males. Many social dances characterized the San Francisco powwow. The show dances done by the San Francisco group consisted almost entirely of the pan-Indian war dances without the unique tribal style furnished by the Sioux in the Oakland group. The Oakland powwow, on the other hand, regularly performed tribal dances and ceremonies. Their war dances were differentiated by tribal styles. They danced fewer social dances. These differences in dance structure seem to be related to the members' views on political activism and to their distinction between a tribal identity and a pan-Indian identity.

Where and when there is a political philosophy that stresses the basic unity of all Indians regardless of tribal affiliation, there tends to be an emphasis on pan-Indian dance forms, forms in which everyone can participate regardless of his or her tribal identity. Where this kind of nationalistic philosophy is lacking or is temporarily ignored, many and varied tribal ceremonies fill the gap and compete with pan-Indian dances to produce a situation where there are criteria for participation that not everyone can meet. Much more investigation must be done before we can make any valid statement about general tendencies, but this comparison of two cases offers an example of what comparison can tell us.

150

16. Sioux dressed for war dance at a Plains encampment

17. Mountain Chief, Blackfoot, in war dance

18. Crow war dance

19. Hopi snake dance. *Photos 16-19 used by permission of the Indiana University Museum, Wesley R. Hurt, Director*

❧ 7 ❧

SYMBOL AND STYLE

A S THE CONTEXT in which dance takes place changes, so must we change our ways of looking at both context and dance. With industrialization, expanding communication networks that shrink the world with each new nonstop flight or orbiting satellite, and population explosions that create urban conglomerates overnight, come changes in nonmaterial aspects of culture, of which dance is one. People have not stopped dancing; they have simply changed the form of the dances they do, and in many cases they do these altered dances for different reasons. I take exception to those who argue that dance becomes less significant with increasing technological complexity. I do agree that dance in complex societies is significant for different reasons than it is in nonliterate societies. Snyder argues that in nonliterate societies dance functions in many of the same ways as a written language would: to teach, to preserve knowledge, and so on.

> Dance functions in some cultures, the non-literate cultures, with as broad a spectrum of functions as the written word includes for others ... dance, in the ritual setting *is* a literature of the non-literate cultures (*in* Comstock, 1974:213-14).

154

It is important here to stress that what happens through the medium of dance is not identical to what happens through the medium of language. If dance does convey meaning, it does not do it in the same way as language, nor can meaning conveyed in the dance be readily translated into words. Hieb makes the point by quoting Isadora Duncan: "If I could tell you what it meant, there would be no point in dancing it" (*in* Comstock, 1974:226). What is it about dance that makes people choose it sometimes over all other modes of expressive behavior? Conversely, why is dance the form most readily and heartily condemned in the clash of cultures? Simply put, why dance? Before returning to these questions, we should determine the different purposes to which dance is put in complex societies. One of the more important uses is that of dance as an identity marker. With the shrinking of the spatial world through better communication and the expanding of it through population increase, there are few societies left that have the luxury of isolation. It is not true, however, that people, having been brought into contact with others, have melded into a great homogeneous mass and lost their respective identities in the process. On the contrary, in many instances it is precisely this contact, opposition, or rivalry that leads to a stronger maintenance or revival of identity.

Within anthropology there was a shift in emphasis that involved the difference between looking at discrete units of people as entities unto themselves and looking at the relationships between individuals and between groups of individuals. Out of this new focus grew an interest in the ways in which some groups are able to maintain a consistent identity while other groups lose their identity under similar circumstances. Both Barth and Spicer cite opposition as one of these mechanisms, Spicer making the stronger case for it:

> Tentatively, on the basis of our limited data, it appears that the oppositional process is the essential factor in the formation and development of the persistent identity system. . . . The opposi-

tional process frequently produces intense collective consciousness and a high degree of internal solidarity. This is accompanied by a motivation for individuals to continue the kind of
experience that is "stored" in the identity system in symbolic
form (1971:797,799).

Interaction between relative strangers or between those who
do not share all the same cultural knowledge is fraught with
problems. As Monica Wilson indicates, "When people of different languages and cultures interact, failures of communication
are legion" (*in* LaFontaine, 1972:197). What we find happening
is that interaction becomes structured in such a way that it takes
place in terms of stereotypes:

> When native and non-native users of a culture interact, they
> typically do so in terms of stereotyped, ethnocentric, and over-
> simplified views of each other; given the narrowness of the
> common universe of cultural discourse, interaction is much
> more limited in scope and complexity than between native users
> (Colby and Van Den Berghe, 1969:23).

Interacting at this level removes some of the danger by ritualiz-
ing the proceedings. The interaction is also frequently limited
to formal situations, which again are easier to control.

Identity markers that mark off one group from another
must necessarily be recognized as symbolizing the group both
by the group members themselves and by members of other
groups. So that there is no blurring of boundaries, the symbols
employed are generally immediately recognizable and unmis-
takably signify one particular group. This is where stereotypes
play an important role in interaction. Stereotypes pick out one
or two features of an individual or group and emphasize them,
thus producing a kind of caricature or larger-than-life representation.

Sometimes stereotypes applied derisively by one group to
another are taken over by the group to whom they are applied
and incorporated into the complex of identity symbols. "Yankee Doodle" is a well-known example. The term was originally

applied by a British army surgeon to some regiments of the Continental army known for their flashy, somewhat *outré* uniforms. One of the early verses of the song has a line that goes, "stuck a feather in his cap and called it macaroni." The reference here is to a group of English fops who wore enormous powdered wigs with bunches of curls, ribbons, and feathers as well as very short, full coats. Because the style was borrowed from Italian fashion of the time, these gentlemen referred to themselves as "macaronis." At any rate, the epithet "Yankee Doodle" was soon picked up by the Americans as a symbol of American identity as opposed to any identity with ties to England.

Stereotypes also abound in the realm of dance. Ask a person about Mexican dance and almost certainly he will mention the Mexican hat dance (*Jarabe tapatío*). Asked about American Indian dance, people will respond with images of war-bonneted, feather-bustled Plains Indians doing war dances. In southern Mexico I was asked to teach some "typical" American dances. At a loss as to what they might be, I was informed that what the person had in mind were square dances.

The whole complex of features that people rely on to mark their identity comprises something I have called style. Style, as I define it, is composed of symbols, forms, and underlying value orientations (Royce, 1975:54). Overt forms and symbols include such areas as dress, language, music, dance, house types, and religion. These are buttressed by values such as friendship, the Protestant ethic, and education. This same complex has in the past been most frequently referred to by the word "tradition." The term "tradition," however, implies something conservative and unchanging, while signs, symbols, and values change all the time. We have seen this already in the examples of change in Tongan, Hawaiian, and Balinese dance, and we will see yet another example at the end of this chapter. Tradition also implies that people have no choice about whether or not to break with it. It takes on the aura of some omnipresent institution that dictates the lives of those living within its shadow. This too is an exaggeration. People generally make an active choice about displaying particular styles. Kroeber made this point about the element of selectivity: "There must be alternative choices, though actually they may never be elected. Where compulsion or physiological necessity reign, there is no room for style" (1963:150). People are also constantly in the process of adding some items and discarding others, thus changing the style complex. Additionally, people seem to feel little inhibition about displaying more than one style, and they choose the style appropriate to the situation. When Isthmus Zapotec find themselves in formal situations where they are in the presence of outsiders, they tend to display all the features of Zapotec style. That is, they speak Zapotec, dance *sones,* wear Zapotec regional dress, and so on. When these people are in an informal setting among other Zapotec, they are quite likely to speak Spanish, dance Western-type social dances, and wear Western dress.

Of all the features that make up style complexes, dance is one of the most significant; it is certainly one of the most universal. Dance, it would seem, has great potential for communicating something about how people feel about themselves, particularly in situations where different peoples come in contact. This potential gives dance great power and at the same time makes it threatening. "One of the ironies of culture contact is that each group often regards the art, and particularly the dancing, of the other as *immoral,* as well as distasteful" (Wilson *in* LaFontaine, 1972:194). In the same article Wilson goes on to say that the early missionaries to the Xhosa in South Africa saw that the girls' initiation dance and the boys' circumcision dance were banned by law as being "contrary to good morals." She also points out, however, that many of the South African peoples regarded Western ballroom dancing with its contact between partners as indecent. The same phenomenon characterizes Tongan dance history. The missionaries banned indigenous dance as being lascivious, while we find Tongan girls doing a parody of classical ballet in which they refuse to use

158

their thighs because according to Tongan standards displaying or using one's thighs in dance is indecent (Kaeppler, 1967b). The waltz, in its original form done by South German peasants, was just another dance. When it found its way into court circles, it was viewed as being risqué and not the sort of thing that respectable people would find pleasure in doing. It soon insinuated itself into the programs of assemblies and balls. The waltz is now the acme of respectability and conservatism.

Anything which because of its nature prompts people to ban it must be potent indeed. As we have seen, dance is frequently banned. This brings us back to the questions we have already posed: What is it about dance that gives it its impact as a form of expressive behavior? Is there anything unique about dance that sets it apart from other potential choices of expressive behavior? Can things be said through the vehicle of dance which can be said in no other way?

The factor that underlies all potential answers is that of the human body. The body is the instrument of dance, the medium of expression. This makes dance more immediate in its impact not only for the dancer but for the observer as well. Whether the response be one of enthusiastic approval or disgust or any emotion between the extremes, people always have some response to the body as it is used in dance; they are seldom neutral. One can be neutral toward a painting, a carving, or even a piece of music because they are all forms of expression one step removed from the individual who created them. Additionally, they are lifeless objects, not living, moving human beings. In an attempt to dilute the body's power to incite emotion, we in Western society have hedged it about with social conventions. Kirstein speaks of this in his 1935 book on the dance:

Our civilizing education in the conventions of respectful politeness teaches us not to point, not to laugh too loud, not to leap for joy, not to embrace in the streets. Our demonstrative idiom has been withered from the time when the kings in Israel tore their hair, wept aloud, beating their breasts or throwing themselves

159

on the ground, or when King Charlemagne tore his beard for wrath at the news of Roncevaux. The effect of this withering is most apparent in modern social dances and their practically static positions and movements (1935:3).

In fact, dance provides one of the few opportunities in the modern world for displaying the body that is accepted by society. It gives us an outlet for all the emotion constrained from not pointing, not laughing too loud, not leaping for joy, and not embracing in the streets. Small wonder then that it is a potent symbol.

We have said that dance has a more immediate impact on both performer and spectator because the creation and the creator are one and the same thing. It may also be that part of its impact is due to the fact that it is not bound by the restrictions of language, which is important when strangers interact. Not all gestures are universal either, but they have more of this quality than language does. The master of gesture, the mime Marcel Marceau, has spoken about the distinction between gesture and language:

> Everything can be expressed through the art of mime, which shuns the deceitful words that raise barriers of misunderstanding between men. Words can be deceitful, but the mime, in order to be understood by all, must be simple and clear, without ambiguity. The Greek author, Lucian, has said that "a mime actor who makes a wrong gesture is guilty of a solecism with his hand" (souvenir program, 1975).

In some ways dance reveals more than language and the other arts. Baudelaire has made the point quite nicely, though impressionistically: "Dancing can reveal all the mystery that music conceals" (cited in Beaumont, 1934:16). Why it should reveal more is not quite clear except that it depends on the body. There is some reason to believe that it is harder to lie or conceal through movement than through words or another medium.

160

Laban was perhaps the first to discuss characteristic movement patterns in any systematic way. He proposed that there are recognizable movement styles that vary from society to society and culture to culture: "Communities seem to regard a certain uniformity of movement behavior as indispensable for safeguarding the stability of the community spirit" (cited in Lomax, 1968:236). Strangers are identifiable by the way they move. Southern Zapotec recognize Americans at great distances simply by the fact that they walk briskly with long strides as if they were always in a hurry. Laban then goes on to speak of deception through movement:

> The fact is that man is able to disguise his effort nature as well as his effort patterns to a certain extent. Such a disguise will deceive only an unobservant person, though leaving him with a vague feeling that something is wrong. This feeling results from subconscious observation, or rather from observation not brought to full consciousness (Laban, 1960:113).

This too we know intuitively to be true, having been in situations where a person is saying one thing with words and quite another with posture, gesture, and movement.

An example from observations at a Zapotec wedding will make clear how ingrained movement patterns are. In 1971 a wedding was held between a Zapotec boy from the city of Juchitán and a Mexican girl from the city of Oaxaca. All the female guests from Juchitán were requested to wear the regional costure, which consists of a long, gathered or gored skirt and a short-sleeved overblouse. Many of the women guests did not normally wear the regional costume, preferring the short-skirted Western-style dress, but they came as requested. Everyone was seated in wooden chairs along four sides of a covered area. From my vantage point on one side I suddenly became aware that all of the women who always wear the long-skirted costume were sitting with both feet planted apart and flat on the ground, while the women who usually wear Western dress were sitting with their legs crossed. With a short skirt one

161

cannot sit, with any decorum at least, with one's feet apart and flat on the ground. The normal motor pattern, then, for these women was to cross their legs, and even when they might have sat with legs uncrossed, not one of them did so.

A final word about habitual movement patterns. Much work has recently been done on what is called code-switching in language, that is, where a person switches back and forth between languages or dialects. Research is now being conducted on nonverbal code-switching, or the switching of gestures concomitant with the switching of languages. Preliminary results would appear to indicate that individuals have much more difficulty switching back and forth between gestural systems than they do between languages (Irmgard Bartenieff, personal communication). It may also be that some individuals have more aptitude for switching than others so that, just as some people have an "ear" for languages, others have an "eye" for movement.

Another aspect of dance that may contribute to its potency as a symbol is that it carries information in a number of channels simultaneously. The observer is assaulted with meaning coming from the visual perception of the dancer or dancers, from the accompanying sound that may be produced by musicians or singers or produced by the dancer, from the costuming and masking if any, from the smell of the dancer, and from his or her body heat. All this must be absorbed and processed on the spot, as it were. There is not the luxury of contemplation, as one would have with any of the visual arts. This multisensual immediacy of dance is what contributes to its ability to thrill and excite but also at other times causes people to fear or resent it. Some of us like our catharsis in small doses while others have greater capacities. Some of us hobble our dances so that we are capable only of tiny, mincing steps like the minuet, while others place no encumbrances on the dance and go soaring off in exhibition waltzes. It is when the dance traditions of these two groups come into contact with each other that tension and misunderstanding arise. It is because movement patterns are so ingrained, subconscious for the most part, that we are suspicious of movement patterns that differ from our own. When we are confronted with gestures and ordinary movements that are strange to us, our discomfort remains an unfocused feeling of malaise. We are discomfited by something, but unless we devote some direct thought to it, the source of our unease remains anonymous. When the gesture and movement become reified in the dance, however, then it is a much simpler matter to say precisely what disturbs us, because whatever is there in ordinary movement becomes stylized, bold, and redundant in the dance.

Ultimately, what we can say is that dance is a powerful, frequently adopted symbol of the way people feel about themselves. No one has a foolproof method for predicting which symbols people will seize upon, although there has been considerable discussion of this recently in the debate about communication models. John Blacking, for example, posits a musical mode of communication that conveys information in a manner unlike any other means of communication (1973). Theodore Schwartz, in speaking of ethnic identity and cultural totemism using the Manus of the Admiralty Islands, comments about the selection of symbols of identity. "The Manus, like all other linguistic-ethnic groups in the Admiralties, illustrate the difference—amplifying effect of formally recognizing incipient cultural differences that would seem very small to the outsider, while overlooking (in some contexts) massive commonality" (in De Vos and Romanucci-Ross, 1975:111). Perhaps the most satisfactory statement on the subject was made by Monica Wilson in her essay on ritual change:

> What particular symbols are retained, or borrowed, or transformed depends upon what catches the imagination. A poet's associations always lie within the frame of his experience as a member of a particular society within a given culture, but inside that frame his imagination roves (1972:200).

When dance is used as a symbol of identity, it usually differs qualitatively from dance that is used for recreation. Elsewhere (Royce, 1973) I have referred to these two kinds of dance as formal and informal, primarily for the ease of having a label, but also because these labels do reflect some of the differences. If one examines those multicultural situations where dance functions as an important symbol of identity, one finds a certain pattern emerging with regard to the specific dance types. Dances that fall into the category of formal are those used explicitly as a symbol of identity on occasions when more than one cultural group interacts or when there is a desire to create a feeling of group solidarity even in the absence of outsiders. Because one wishes the highest status possible for one's own group, one generally chooses symbols that will be accorded prestige by both outsiders and members of one's group. We find, therefore, that dances used in this fashion tend to be showpieces.

There are many factors that can contribute toward the effectiveness of a dance as display. Some of them, like costume, attractiveness of the dancers, and spatial arrangement, have nothing directly to do with the form of the dance itself. In many cases, however, the form of these dances differs from that of recreational dances. Formal dances tend to require more technical skill than the average individual in the particular culture possesses. As we have already noted, this is not a trait of dances done for recreation where the purpose is to encourage full participation. Formal dances also tend to conform to both ingroup and out-group stereotypes. This is one explanation for the fact that, while there is an active repertoire of some ninety *sones* for the Zapotec of the Isthmus of Tehuantepec, any program designed to promote Zapotec nationalism invariably selects the same three *sones*, La Sandunga, La Llorona, and La Tortuga. These three are the dances that any non-Zapotec would name if asked about "typical" dances of the Isthmus. They are, significantly, the three dances that the Ballet Folklórico incorporates in its suite "Wedding in Tehuantepec."

Informal dances, or those done for recreation, usually require no more skill than the average person possesses and normally allow for improvisation. Often these dances will follow

164

the trend in popular dances within the larger national context. An example will clarify the distinction between formal and informal dance.

The Sardana dance of Catalonia first appeared as early as the sixteenth century, and in this early form it is described by Kurath (1949) as being a round dance performed by couples with both Roumanian and Greek motifs. In this form it had a restricted geographic distribution, and its performance was limited to relatively few people. During the nineteenth century, however, when Spain was pressuring the Catalans to become part of the Spanish nation (Spicer, 1971), the Sardana underwent changes in both form and distribution and became a symbol of the Catalan people. The change in form is of interest because it involved a greater musical and choreographic complexity that necessitated a skilled dance leader. In this more demanding form the Sardana spread throughout Catalonia and was apparently so effective as a symbol that the Spanish government attempted to suppress its performance. That the government was unsuccessful we can see from the fact that the dance is still performed as the national dance of Catalonia.

Case Study
ZAPOTEC IDENTITY AND DANCE STYLE

Because of its geographic position as the narrowest bit of land between the Gulf of Mexico and the Pacific Ocean as well as its position as the lowest stretch of land between the great mountains and plateaus of central Mexico and the mountains of southern Mexico and Guatemala, the Isthmus of Tehuantepec in southern Mexico has attracted a diverse assortment of cultures from the earliest times for which we have documentation. Today it is still characterized by its heterogeneity. The northern half on the Gulf coast is rapidly industrializing because of vast oil deposits, and therefore it attracts a variety of potential residents. The southern half, or the coastal plains of the Pacific, has some light industry but for the most part relies on agriculture and small business. Its social makeup is, if any-

165

thing, more heterogeneous than that part of the Isthmus to the north.

The city of Juchitán is the largest city in the southern half of the Isthmus and has a population of about thirty-seven thousand, a diverse lot including Isthmus Zapotec, Mexicans, Spaniards, Italians, Japanese, Lebanese, and other Indian groups such as the Huave, Mixe, and Zoque. The Zapotec, who have been there since before the Spanish conquest in 1521, are four fifths of the total. In terms of identification with particular styles, we can divide Juchitán into two groups: the four fifths of the population who adhere to Zapotec style and the remaining fifth which, although heterogeneous in background, all follow Mexican national style to the exclusion of any other. The greatest degree of elaboration for both styles, but especially for the Zapotec, is evidenced by the upper classes, who alone have the wealth required to display the essential elements of the style. The elements of Zapotec style include a facility in the Zapotec language, the regional costume and gold jewelry which must accompany its wearing, Zapotec music, songs, and dances, and the social round of parties and festive occasions highlighted by the more than twenty-six major *velas* (complexes of daytime parties, masses in the parish church, parades, and an all-night dance under a canvas tent).

One unifying characteristic of all these elements is the syncretism they embody. Not one approaches what one might call "pure" Zapotec in origin and composition. In fact, the very complex of these elements seems to have become elaborated as late as the mid-nineteenth century. At this time a propitious combination of factors allowed the inhabitants of Juchitán to give concrete form to their nationalistic fervor, a trait that had characterized them for at least the preceding three centuries. These factors included the prosperity brought by speculators connected with the trans-Isthmian railroad and the ever-increasing rivalry with the city of Tehuantepec. Many of the elements of Zapotec style were already part of Juchitán life and simply became elaborated and more important. It was no

166

longer sufficient to speak Zapotec on a day-to-day basis; now one composed poetry and songs in it; the traditional skirt and blouse acquired an overlay of French *haut couture* in the form of fine embroidery, velvet, silk, and lace; with the increased wealth, gold jewelry became more and more ostentatious, with fifty-dollar U.S. gold pieces hanging from gold chains and bracelets; the *velas,* which probably had their origin in the fiestas of cooperative societies with religious charters, took on the aspect of European balls. A passage from Covarrubias' *Mexico South* conveys the sense of extravagance, luxury, and Old World tradition:

> To entertain Porfirio [Diaz] on his visits to his beloved Tehuantepec in the manner to which he was accustomed, she [Doña Juana C. Romero] built a "chalet," the only European, two-storied dwelling in town to this day. Great balls were given in his honor, and Diaz seldom missed the yearly *vela bini* given by Doña Juana in a specially built "ballroom," an enclosure of white and gold wooden columns, roofed by a great canvas canopy and hung with crystal chandeliers. It was compulsory to dress for the *vela bini*—the women in the ceremonial Tehuantepec costume of lace, spangles and fringe of gold, which Porfirio preferred; the men in black serge suits and stiff collars despite the unbearable heat . . . Doña Juana gave out little carnets with pencils attached for the guests to write beforehand the partners with whom they would dance lancers, polkas, and waltzes. A great supper was served, with rows of roast turkeys, platters of cold cuts and rivers of imported wine. (1946:233-34).

As the passage above indicates, the Porfirian period in Mexican history (1876-1910) had the most foreign influences since the colonial period when Spain ruled the country. Of all the European countries with interests in Mexico, France was the most influential and extended the influence she had begun in the 1860s during the reign of Maximilian and Carlotta. It is not surprising, then, that Zapotec style should show a predisposition toward things French, since it was during the Porfirian period that the style crystallized.

Zapotec dance proved no exception to foreign, particularly French, influences. The *son,* regarded as Zapotec rather than Mexican, as it developed in the mid-nineteenth century and as it is danced today by members of the old Zapotec families of Juchitán, combines a variety of elements. It is an open-couple dance, which makes it of a later vintage than round dances or line dances. The woman's part incorporates the erect, almost arched-back posture reminiscent of the Andalusian fandango, while the steps themselves remind one of nineteenth-century waltzes. The arm movements are restricted to raising the full skirt on alternate sides. The upper arms remain close to the body, good dancers never allowing their elbows to lose contact with the torso. The skirt is then grasped in each hand. When the dancer moves toward the right, then the right hand raises the skirt until the angle between upper arm and forearm is about 45°; the left hand still grasping the skirt is down so that the arm makes almost a straight line from shoulder to hand and parallel to the body. The movement of the arms reverses with the reversal of direction. The effect of all this is to show off the costume with its heavily embroidered, full velvet skirt and multiple starched white lacy petticoats while giving the dancers that languid, haughty, restrained quality that suits the Juchiteco character so well—a quality which, by the way, is lost in the Ballet Folklórico version. The feet glide across the surface of the floor in a step, step, step close, step, step, step, step back with a half turn so that one is facing in the direction from which one has come, close. This is done in an almost imperceptible semicircle with weight shifts resembling those of a waltz. The direction is then reversed. This deceptively simple-looking step sequence is continued throughout the refrain. Just before the faster *zapateado* (heel work) section begins, the partners change positions with each other, again using the same step. For the woman there is no change of step during the *zapateado,* the same pattern being done slightly faster. Most *sones* have three or four refrain-*zapateado* sequences.

Both in costume and choreography, the woman conveys a thoroughly European quality. The man, on the contrary, is thoroughly Indian. His traditional costume of white cotton shirt and baggy pants, sandals, sombrero, and red neckerchief is like that of almost every other Indian or peasant group in Mexico. His posture, bent slightly forward from the waist with knees relaxed and one or both hands clasped behind his back, is the posture typical of Mexican Indian dance. His steps too are the typical modified *zapateado* found all over rural Mexico.

Many more women regularly dance *sones* than men, and a continuous tradition of teaching *sones* is more formalized among women than among men. Thus it is quite common for women to dance with women. There are also many occasions where only women are in attendance. When women dance with women, both dance the female part.

It is difficult to describe the impact that a performance of *sones* has upon non-Zapotec. At the annual festival of song and dance in the state capital, Oaxaca City, the delegation of dancers from the Isthmus of Tehuantepec always performs next to last, just before the semi-professional group from the university. In spite of the fact that the audience has been sitting on hard wooden benches for the better part of five hours under a searing, white sun, the entrance of the Zapotec delegation never fails to draw gasps of wonder and admiration. Then a hush falls over the crowd, which remains unbroken until the end of the dancing when the audience breaks into wild applause. This kind of reaction is a tribute to the powerful symbolism of the Zapotec performance. Compared to all the groups that have gone before, the Zapotec are unique and unexpected. Unexpected because they are not out of the Oaxaca Indian mold of homespun cotton or woolen costumes and heavy, earthbound, repetitious dances that are done by men and women in the bent-from-the-waist posture with downcast eyes. The sense of wealth and pride is what is conveyed at one's first glimpse of the Zapotec women striding regally onto the

169

dance floor with the enormous, starched and pleated white lace headdresses set back from their faces and the lush, flower-embroidered velvet skirts and blouses providing a background for the thousands of pesos worth of gold jewelry hanging heavily from ears, necks, and wrists. Nothing in the dances that follow contradicts this first impression; rather, it is strengthened as the dancers glide through the *sones* with arrogant graciousness. The whole performance conjures up and reaffirms the image of the proud, fierce, wealthy Zapotec who manage through their wealth and shrewdness to maintain Juchitán as a Zapotec city.

Sones are not danced only at the annual festival in Oaxaca City. Most fiestas in Juchitán are characterized by the dancing of *sones*. There are some occasions when *sones* seem almost to be mandatory, usually whenever there is a threat felt from the outside or from outsiders. Most often this occurs within the context of a Zapotec–non-Zapotec marriage. At the Sunday celebration of mixed marriages it is not unusual for the women guests to be requested to wear the regional costume rather than the long dresses or pants suits they might otherwise wear. Often the hosts will hire flute and drum players to play the oldest form of music still heard in Juchitán, although normally this type of music is no longer played at weddings. Many more *sones* are danced than usual; in fact, they outnumber the popular Mexican social dances that are generally the predominant fare at weddings. In other words, Zapotec style is explicitly displayed so that the friends and relatives of the outsider spouse will be impressed with extravagance and richness of the Zapotec heritage, which can more than hold its own in competition with anything else Mexico has to offer.

Any occasion where non-Zapotec are present may call forth this same display of style. In addition there are also displays of Zapotec identity when no outsiders are in evidence. One occurred in 1971 on the occasion of a victory dance given to celebrate a local candidate winning the municipal presidency after running on a Juchitán-for-the-Juchitecos ticket under the aus-

170

pices of the Popular Socialist Party. The women all came in their finest costumes hung about with fortunes in gold. Two of the five bands hired for the occasion played nothing but *sones* all evening, and the other three alternated between *sones* and *piezas,* the modern popular music.

One also sees magnificent exhibitions of Zapotec style during the *velas* sponsored by two of the oldest families of Juchitán. Each of the families would like to be considered the finest embodiment of all that is Zapotec, and they attempt to outdo each other in their respective *velas.*

Zapotec identity is also a primary feature of celebrations associated with important events in local history. For example, the victory of the Juchiteco forces over the French army with its regiment of traitors from Tehuantepec on September 5, 1866, is celebrated each year with a municipal dance where Zapotec dress is de riguer, and those who come in Western dress must sit in the back rows.

Otherwise, one is quite as likely to see *piezas* being danced as *sones.* Many of the Zapotec pride themselves on being excellent performers of the latest social dances. Latest, however, usually implies a time lag, so that at the beginning of the twentieth century the waltz was popular; this was followed by the *danzón* in the thirties and forties; that was superseded in the fifties and sixties by the *cumbia* and the twist; and today *música tropical* and the dances that accompany it such as the cha cha, samba, and mambo enjoy preeminence. Being expert in the two distinct dance traditions is a source of pride, and it certainly causes no conflict of loyalties. Both the reasons for doing each form of dance and the occasions on which they are done are different, and the Zapotec are accustomed to making the appropriate selection for each situation.

Zapotec dance is an effective symbol of the pride in a Zapotec heritage mainly because in all respects it connotes aristocracy. The choreography and posture are regal and unhurried; the required costume is lavish and costly; finally, the skill required to dance well in the Zapotec fashion can be acquired

20. Zapotec woman from Juchitán dancing "La Sandunga" at the Guelaguetza

21. Zapotec couples from Juchitán coming on stage at the Guelaguetza

22: Zapotec women at the "repartido de pan" for the Vela Pineda in Juchitán

23. Zapotec women dancing a *son* at the "repartido de pan" for the Vela Pineda. *Photos by A. and R. Royce*

only through imitation and practice. This means that fine dancers belong to the Zapotec elite because it is those families who began the tradition and who have the money to maintain it. Any Zapotec can dance *sones* but only those few with access to the tradition can dance them well.

PART THREE

Future Directions

❧ 8 ❧

THE MORPHOLOGY
OF DANCE

IN CHAPTER 4, I spoke about two emphases that characterized the anthropology of dance, the emphasis on form
and the emphasis on function. Most research illustrates these
emphases, focusing either on the morphology of the dance or
on its place within the broader context. We have seen in Chapter 4 on structure and function what past and present research
is like in these two specific areas, and from that knowledge we
can see the kinds of foundations both structural and functional
studies have laid. Just as this basic dichotomy has underlain
previous research, so will it determine the nature of future
research.

In this chapter we will be concerned with potential research
that rests ultimately on the structure of dance. Two areas have
relevance to a great many disciplines within the humanities and
the sciences to which the anthropology of dance can make a
significant contribution. They are aesthetics and creativity as
culturally determined. One way of approaching both of them is
through structural analysis. Looking at the two concepts from
the perspective we have outlined means that we are not con-

cerned with individual aesthetic judgments or with cases of individual creativity. The area about which we, as anthropologists of the dance, may speak from a position of authority is that of a culture's aesthetic values and a culture's determination of creativity. Once we have done this for single cultures, we may then compare cultures and, ultimately, speak of cross-cultural variation in both aesthetics and creativity. As Merriam indicated in his discussion of aesthetics and the interrelationship of the arts (1964), most of what has been said about aesthetics (and I would also add creativity) derives from Western concepts of art. Not much has changed since 1964 in terms of actual studies or theoretical statements, but the concern for finding a different approach exists. Anthropologists have the means as well as the concern in that they have developed cross-cultural methodologies which attempt to avoid culture-bound biases regardless of whose they are. The anthropology of dance, more so even than other subareas of anthropology, has both means and background to make statements founded on research about aesthetics and creativity as they apply to dance. That we have not yet done so is simply because we need to have the tools of structural analysis applied and tested. Knowing now that structural analysis is possible and having several good examples of it, we may use it as it should be used, as a tool, as a means to an end.

Aesthetic judgments are basically the set of rules a culture has that bind artistic activity. Creativity involves an intimate knowledge of those rules so that one may then bend them, disregard them momentarily, and break them—all within cultural limits. Obviously there is a feedback between the two since the cumulative product of creativity is a new aesthetic, new, however, only in the sense that it is ever-changing and evolving. I do not think that we need consider the individuals who are so creative that their creations are totally unacceptable within their own culture. Their efforts will have little or no impact on dance within a cultural context. The cultural context is the only subject about which the anthropologist can claim special license to speak. Individuals who are creative out of their own time and who are belatedly recognized (assuming that their own time allows them to continue making artistic statements at all) are more appropriately viewed by art historians or biographers than by anthropologists.

It would seem that there are two ways in which one may approach the concept of aesthetics and retain cross-cultural validity. The first of them, as exemplified by Thompson's work, particularly *African Art in Motion* (1974), involves intensive questioning of many participants in a particular art form (by participants is meant both observers and performers) using both live performance and stimulus material in the form of video tape and photographs as a basis for questions. What this attempts to elicit is a sort of ethnoaesthetic. Thompson states that his purpose is to extract the "criteria of fine form which seem to be shared among makers of sculpture, music, and the dance" (1974:xii). The fact that there are flaws in the methodology of this particular study (see Hanna, 1974-75) does not invalidate the basic approach. As Hanna suggests, what are first needed are these kinds of studies carefully documented for single cases. If and when cross-cultural comparisons are attempted, then the canons of cross-cultural research must be met.

In the normal course of doing fieldwork, one encounters a number of opportunities for collecting this kind of information, that is, standards by which dance and dance performance is judged. If one is being taught dances, one learns criteria by being corrected or by being told to watch a certain person who is considered to be a fine dancer. Opportunities abound for learning aesthetic values at performances of dance. If the people do not have a tradition of criticism, critical appraisals can be elicited without prejudicing the responses. Once one has constructed the skeleton of an aesthetic system in this manner, one can flesh it out by devising systematic questionnaires. Another advantage to proceeding slowly and by degrees is that by the time you are ready to construct a questionnaire not only will you know what the appropriate questions are but you will also know who the appropriate people are to ask. Once you have gone through this procedure for dance, you might wish to extend it to other forms of expressive behavior to determine whether one may speak of a single aesthetic applicable to art in general within that group, whether each form has a different set of criteria by which it is judged, or whether there are clusters of art forms which are judged by the same standards.

The second way one might approach the question of aesthetics is through structural analysis. To my knowledge this has not yet been done either for dance or for any other form of expressive behavior. It would seem, nonetheless, an ideal approach since what this type of analysis offers is a "grammar" of the dance, in other words, rules for combining dance elements that when followed will produce total dances that are culturally acceptable. In societies with more than one dance type, there may be more than one aesthetic, but this too may be determined through structural analysis. There is also a difference between dances which are merely culturally acceptable and those which are outstanding. The differences between a dance that meets minimal standards and a dance that goes beyond may be pinpointed through structural analysis. Structural formulae, such as those suggested by György Martin and Ernö Pésovar (1961), facilitate comparison because, unlike notation or verbal descriptions, they allow one to see differences at a glance.

A criticism that some might make of approaching aesthetics this way is that it does not require that criteria be verbalized. That is, if standards and evaluative criteria are not articulated by a people, then we cannot speak of an aesthetic for them. This, I think, is a false notion which arises from our thinking of art and aesthetics solely in Western terms. It is probably accurate to say that most people will be able to state preferences for one or another of different examples of the same artistic genre. The choice need not be based on such Western concepts as beauty. For example, one dance may be preferred over another because it is older or because it is more efficacious in a particular ritual. In the absence of studies directed toward cross-cultural aesthetics which would meet standards of ethnographic adequacy, it is certainly not valid to dismiss out of hand the notion of a non-Western aesthetic.

That people make choices with regard to dances is evident if you look at the dance repertoire of any given group over a given time. The fact is that some dances are retained while others are dropped. Over extended periods this reflects changes in aesthetic preferences. In addition, we have the nonacceptance of specific dances that do not meet the aesthetic principles in operation at the time they are introduced. Moreover, there are differences in dance repertoires with regard to stability. Some dance types, because of their structure, allow a great deal of improvisation, thereby providing more opportunities for innovation. In them, one would have the greatest opportunity of observing day-to-day aesthetic preferences. It is also possible that they are correlated with a more active, perhaps more verbalized, aesthetic. (Hungarian dance has this kind of structure.) Other dance repertoires emphasize verbatim passing on of dances and rigidly exclude innovation. This is particularly true of dances embedded in ritual contexts.

If we define aesthetics as a set of criteria which, if followed, will produce an artistic expression that is culturally acceptable, then we may define creativity as that quality which allows an individual to recombine criteria or go beyond them to produce an artistic expression that is "new" but still culturally acceptable. A definition of creativity that is comparable, although it speaks specifically to creativity in science, is that proposed by Maugh (1974), who refers to it as "that ill-defined state of mind which allows the investigator to forge anomalous or apparently unrelated facts into bold new chains of theory" (1273).

As with aesthetics, we already have a foundation for looking at creativity within a cultural context in the form of structural analysis. Using structural analysis, we can see what the cultural limitations placed on creativity are, how the creative individual works, and also what kinds of outside elements are likely to be

181

accepted. Structural analysis can tell us what creativity is with reference to the dance of a specific group, but it cannot predict the precise forms creativity will take. Neither can it tell us why specific individuals are creative or how to create creativity.

Individual creativity and how to encourage it were recently the subject of a symposium that brought together individuals acknowledged to be creative in the hopes that they might shed some light upon the subject. The questions remained largely unanswered. Some conclusions of consequence for our purposes were reached, however. Sir Karl Popper suggested that creativity can be divided into two stages, the first that of obtaining ideas, and the second that of criticizing those ideas to separate the worthless ones from the worthwhile. He then went on to comment that the first stage cannot be taught or cultivated, while the second can be developed through education (*in* Maugh, 1974:1273). With regard to dance, it is precisely this first stage of individual creativity and its source about which we, as anthropologists studying the dance, can say nothing.

At the same symposium Leon Eisenberg made the important point that, since the creative process is for most people a preverbal one, translating that process into words changes one's perceptions of the process: "Many conclusions drawn from this verbal reconstruction of the creative process may be incorrect if the reconstruction is itself faulty" (*in* Maugh, 1974:1273). If instead we asked people to tell us which dance elements they combined and why, the phenomenon might easily be distorted. It is perfectly feasible, for example, for a person to build up a dance in units that do not have names. If then asked to articulate the choreographic process, one would have to do so in terms of named units. Doing so in this case would distort the process. Structural analysis to a certain extent eliminates the necessity of verbalizing what takes place when dances are being composed.

What can structural analysis tell us about creative choreographers? By looking at the structure of the dances they create, we can see exactly how it is that they combine the standard elements of the particular dance form so as to create a dance that is new in its use of old elements. The choreographer here works in ways analogous to those Maugh posits for the scientist when he speaks of forging anomalous and apparently unrelated facts into new chains of theory.

This is one of the ways in which creativity occurs in choreography. Although there are probably other formulae for introducing change in dance styles, three seem to characterize much of what we may consider creative choreography:

1. Recombination of traditional elements in new ways,
2. Introduction of new elements,
3. Change in the length of the basic dance phrase.

The first two can be and have been documented for a variety of dance traditions. The third represents an area in which research and documentation still remain to be done.

For the moment let us look at the first two kinds of choreographic creativity, taking the ballet as an example. Once the classic technical vocabulary of ballet became set, the ballet was characterized by conservatism with regard to change of the second type, that is, the introduction of new elements. The history of the ballet, however, has been anything but conservative, and most of the change and ferment have been due to creativity of the first kind, the reworking of traditional dance elements.

The ballet has always been characterized by two different emphases, one on movement and the other on story or plot. Much of the dramatic change in choreographic styles has resulted from oscillation between the two or of recombining them in new ways. At the end of the seventeenth century the *ballet à entrée* reigned. It was a form that saw the dance as essentially subservient to music and drama. It was, as its name implies, a piece of fluff between acts of the more serious business of the theater. Emphasis was on the movement itself and on the virtuosity of the performers. Ballet in this form was designed to display technique. Any story line would have defeated the purpose of the *entracte*. The eighteenth century saw a rise of the

183

ballet d'action, which stressed the importance of dramatic unity in the ballet. The earliest example of this genre which made use of neither song nor speech was Weaver's "The Loves of Mars and Venus," staged in 1717, but the real master of the dramatic ballet was Noverre. In the process of creating dramatic ballets, Noverre also initiated many innovations that have implications even for the ballet of today. Among other things, he held that "ballets should be unified works of art in which every element contributes to the development of the main theme, that technical exhibitions for their own sake should be discouraged, and that such impediments to movement and expression as heeled shoes and cumbersome skirts should be abolished" (Anderson, 1974:35).

The emphasis on story remained throughout the late eighteenth century in the dramatic ballets of Viganò such as "Richard Coeur de Lion," "Joan of Arc," "Othello" and "Coriolanus" (Anderson, 1974:39). One of the old elements that was reintroduced in the ballets of this type was the use of mime. The mid-nineteenth-century romantic era in ballet retained the idea of drama, though the preference changed from drama on a heroic scale (which used many classical themes) to drama that utilized folk themes and emotional expression. Three of the ballets from this period are still mainstays of many repertoires, "La Sylphide," "Giselle," and "Coppélia."

The pendulum swung back in the direction of dance for movement's sake with the influence of Marius Petipa at the end of the nineteenth century. His innovations lay primarily in the direction of reintroducing virtuoso technique and combining such elements as mime, folk themes, and the lyricism of romantic ballet in new ways. Certainly we may speak of creativity when we consider his great formulaic ballets, "Raymonda," "La Bayadére," "Sleeping Beauty," and, with Ivanov, "Nutcracker" and "Swan Lake." The significant elements of Petipa's formula include the matching of dancing styles with character types, from which we derive the categories of *danseur noble* and *caractère;* the obligatory scene of divertissements, which provided the setting for brilliant showpieces of pure dance; the use of standardized mime sequences; the pas de deux with its unvarying pattern of adagio, male variation, female variation, and coda; and the length of the ballet itself, stretching usually over three acts. Anderson describes the Petipa style in a way that conveys both its distinctiveness and its incorporation of traditional components.

> Filled with mime, dramatic dance, lyric dance, classical dance, character dance, and *divertissements*, Petipa's ballets were essentially panoramic. . . . Petipa constructed whole universes of movement in which each separate dance glittered like a star yet formed part of a harmonious whole. Indeed, glittering is a good adjective to describe Petipa's works, for he replaced the softness and fragility of Romantic ballet with a diamond-edged sharpness (1974:67).

The Petipa tradition was not carried forward by choreographers in the early part of the twentieth century. In fact, drama and story similar to what was popular in the romantic era were characteristic of those choreographers rebelling against the conventions of Petipa and Ivanov. The Ballet Russes searched far afield for its folk themes, so that in its repertoire we find Asia replacing the sylph-haunted, moonbeam-strewn glades of the Black Forest. Not that the use of exotic material from the Orient was new. Noverre in 1754 incorporated Oriental themes in "Les Fêtes Chinoises," one of his first successes. Story was definitely emphasized over pure movement in the early years of the twentieth century and for a variety of reasons: first, it was in part a reaction to the Russian ballet establishment; second, troupes of dancers, such as the Ballet Russes, simply did not have the wherewithal in terms of dancers, settings, or theaters to continue the Russian tradition; and third, the times were such that the unusual in theme, whether it was Russian folk tale, classical mythology, or psychological drama, was sought and acclaimed.

In the contemporary ballet we have once again returned to movement rather than plot. As Kirstein stated in 1952, the contemporary classical ballet depends on what survives from nineteenth-century dance rather than from the creations of the early part of this century. Contemporary choreographers start from the foundation of the classic tradition, and it is of interest that Balanchine, whom public opinion holds to be one of the most creative choreographers of this century, does not consider himself innovative or original.

> The subject of Balanchine's ballets, apart from love (of music, of the human body, of human beings) is the physical act or presence of the dance itself, not "abstractly," for the sake of detached, desiccated, or decorative motion, but concretely, representing and demonstrating the conscious mechanism in its preparation and animation through mastery of time, space, and gesture (Kirstein, 1951:17).

There exist other kinds of recombinations of elements that make one choreographer distinct from another and that lead the public to consider him innovative. Though Balanchine considers himself to be no more innovative than anyone working in the classic tradition, part of his innovation comes from the fact that he abandoned the Petipa formula and at the same time returned to the Petipa emphasis on movement, virtuosity, and the line of the body.

Bournonville, a nineteenth-century choreographer and ballet master, certainly developed a distinctive and innovative style based on fast, intricate footwork and ballon (a light, springy quality). Anderson gives a rather intriguing explanation for these innovations:

> Some of these qualities may stem from Bournonville's attempts to hide his own personal defects. He had a brittle way of landing his jumps and he tried to disguise this by inventing sequences in which the landing is followed not by a sustained pose—which would permit spectators to scrutinize him for faults—but by an immediate take-off into another movement. The resultant Bournonville style emphasizes elevation and strength in its steps for men, sweetness and charm in its steps for women (1974:46).

The same rationale for innovation by reworking could be applied to much of what was new in the choreography of Filippo Taglioni (1778-1871). His daughter was his star pupil and much of his choreography was designed for her. As her arms were rather long, he modified the standard *port du bras* so that her arms were shown off to their best advantage rather than seen as a liability. She was also a naturally light, ethereal dancer, and, to make the best use of this, Taglioni père eliminated coquettish, vivacious movements from his choreography and stressed instead those movements which conveyed the supernatural, the virginal, the ethereal.

The romantic era glorified the ballerina and relegated the male to the role of attendant. Prior to this period, another of the ballet's most creative choreographers, Didelot (1767-1836), in his development of the pas de deux emphasized and utilized the differences in male and female dance qualities—the male being strong in support, lifts, and jumps, and the female being quick and light (Kirstein, 1970:130). Before Didelot the male reigned supreme.

Much of Balanchine's creativity lies in the realm of his dignifying the role of the male dancer. In fact, if one looks carefully at what is distinctive about much of Balanchine's choreography, it is the emphasis on the male dancer and the transference of the male qualities of strength, speed, ballon, and spareness of line to Balanchine's female dancers.

If we look at the history of the ballet, we can readily discern trends and changes in fashion, such as pure movement versus storytelling movement and male qualities versus female qualities. With this knowledge we can anticipate the directions the creative choreographer or dancer may take. The same, of course, would be true of any dance form for which we have any time depth. Hungarian dance, for example, would make an interesting study since we have good diachronic material. What we are assuming here is a relative consistency in the way styles change. What the model does not allow us to anticipate with any degree of success is the once-in-a-lifetime creative act that af-

187

fects all subsequent acts of creativity. Such a unique event in the ballet was the introduction of the toe slipper. This is an example of the second mode of creative change, the introduction of new elements.

The blocked toe shoe must certainly be one of the most significant new elements to be introduced into the ballet. Its appearance was preceded by the use of wires and stage machinery that gave the impression of airiness and flight. One of the more memorable uses of machinery was the Didelot production of "Flore et Zéphyre" in 1815, which managed to conceal the apparatus so ingeniously that it was invisible to the audience; Kirstein describes the effect:

> Alone, apart, without any followers to distract the attention, he (Zéphyre) rises from the center of the stage by his own strength; with disdainful foot he spurns the earth he forsakes, soars for several minutes [sic] into space, grazes with the tips of his wings the greenish tops of the trees, and at last majestically disappears amid the azure vault. . . . Applause was prolonged far into the interval and broke out with redoubled vigor when Zéphyre, returning in the same way he ascended, rose a second time bearing Flore in his arms" (cited in Kirstein, 1970:131).

By the 1830s, the use of the stitched or blocked toe shoe was well established. It not only enabled the ballerina to simulate an airy quality, but it also made possible a number of other changes. Kirstein enumerates some of them:

> At the start, poses were only momentarily sustained, but once the principle was established, enormous development was possible both for the ballerina and male dancer. She turned more brilliantly on *pointe;* he could turn her more rapidly; profiles in combination became more extended (ibid.:131).

The new shoe was as significant as the innovation of turning out the legs and feet that preceded it by at least one century. Just as turning out enormously increased movement possibilities, so did the use of the toe shoe make hitherto impossible movements possible.

I do not think that the ballet is unique in relying almost entirely on the first kind of creativity, that is, the reworking of elements already in the tradition. The creative individual, whatever the medium, still must work within the bounds of cultural tradition if the creation is to find acceptance as part of that tradition's inventory. In dance it seems easier for people to accept change if it comes in the form of traditional elements presented in new ways. In addition, of course, is the universal truth that creating a totally new form or idea is a relatively rare phenomenon.

The third possibility for creativity in the dance is changing the length of the basic dance phrases. To my knowledge no one has begun to investigate the possibility that choreographers known for their innovative abilities may introduce new styles in dance by lengthening or shortening the dance phrase typical of their dance tradition. That these basic dance phrases exist and can be ascertained through structural analysis is a reasonable assumption based on the work of both Martin and Kaeppler discussed previously with reference to structural analysis. Both have analyzed dance structure and have been able to point to minimum phrases of movement and to minimum meaningful phrases. One could arrive at the most usual or comfortable size of phrase by observing individuals choreographing dance. A research design for this might involve videotaping a choreographer at work, which would produce a record from which one could see the size of the building blocks of the dance, as it were. Then, assuming the information is available that lets one determine who are considered innovative choreographers and who are the ones working more closely within the tradition, one could compare the choreographic process. This comparison would allow one to determine whether choreographers are creative because of the use of atypical phrase lengths or because of their use of atypical sequences of dance elements. This, in turn, could reveal directions creativity might take.

It may be that the culturally appropriate movement phrase is something extremely conservative, just as Laban has described culturally appropriate posture to be, and that, just as an

189

individual's cultural identity can be ascertained quickly and easily from posture, so can this identity be determined by use of a particular length of phrase. Some mimetic dances rely on caricatures of postural styles to communicate identity of the characters in the dance. In the same way, caricatures of phrases may also be used to communicate identity. An excellent example of the distortion of typical phrase lengths can be seen in the Twyla Tharp choreography to music of Handel, "As Time Goes By." In this satirical piece Tharp extends movements far beyond their ordinary length or else cuts them off in mid-phrase. The result of this convention-breaking is a truly superb satire on traditional ballet.

Whether investigation reveals phrase length to be a conservative and rarely invoked means of creativity in the dance or to be an alternative frequently employed, this area of research is one that promises to be fruitful not only for the study of creativity but also for what it can tell us about cross-cultural variations in movement style. Since we have already begun to investigate the other two modes of introducing new dance styles, and since they have already been well documented in the area of cultural change in general, it would be foolish to ignore the third possible creative mode. It may well be that what would be relatively simple to document for dance may have implications for creativity in general.

Structural analysis, developing initially out of the desire to preserve and understand the form of dances, has clearly demonstrated its enormous potential for elucidating the two related areas of aesthetics and creativity. These are areas that have long tempted and puzzled investigators to the extent that we can point to a wealth of impressionistic statements about both of them. We have now the foundations from which to go beyond impressionistic statements. Once we know the structure of a dance style, we can begin to say something about aesthetic preferences. From that, we can then speak about frameworks within which creativity takes place. By observing how dancers and choreographers work within a dance style and at the same time introduce change, by seeing how they manipulate the limits of the culturally allowable, we see both what the rules for artistic judgments are, aesthetics, and how the rules are sometimes set aside, creativity.

❧ 9 ❧

THE
MEANING OF DANCE

W HEN WE SPEAK of the meaning of dance, we are implicitly comparing the communicative aspects of dance behavior with other media of expression. We are asking what is it about the expressive capacities of dance that sometimes makes it the most effective conveyor of meaning. Until quite recently, however, most statements about dance and communication have not gone beyond the impressionistic analogy between dance and language. The analogy assumes that dance functions in the same way as language and has the same capacities. I would not deny that this is possible, and I offer the following example of dance used literally and figuratively as a language.

> The age delighted in allegory, and some of the figures thus formed came to have symbolical meanings. An account of 1610 states that the triangle symbolized Justice, three circles conjoined meant Truth Known, a square within a square was Virtuous Design, and three circles within one another stood for Perfect Truth. Dancers could also form letters of the alphabet or words.

Thus, for example, in *Salmacida Spolia,* an English masque of 1640, nymphs spelled out "Anna Regina," referring to Anne of Denmark, Mother of Charles I (Anderson, 1974:16-17).

Although the dancers in the above example managed to convey precisely the same message as if spoken or written words had been used, their feat was by no means as economical. Most of the impressionistic statements about dance as language, however, were not referring to a literal usage. They spoke, rather, about gesture and steps in vague and lofty ways. The following quatrain by Delille is representative of its genre:

> Que la danse toujours, ou gaie ou serieuse,
> Soit de nos sentimens l'image ingénieuse;
> Que tous ses mouvemens du coeur soient les échos;
> Ses gestes un language, et ses pas des tableaux!
>
> (cited in Beaumont, 1934:41)

Progress toward appreciation of the communicative aspects of dance can be seen in statements which suggest that it is a mistake to expect dance to serve the same functions as language. It is a mistake, first, because dance is inferior to language for that kind of communication, and, second, because using it in this way means that its true expressive capabilities are being slighted, as Marcel Marceau observes when he contrasts mime and dance:

> When dance tries to express anecdotes with pantomime, it is as a sort of deaf and dumb language, with gestures that are almost theatrical—naturalistic—and that is why Balanchine has denuded classical dance of all the useless chattering, to keep it in beautiful pure lines. It is this sort of deaf-mute gesturing that pantomime has systematically rejected, to deal, instead, in symbolism (1975:36).

Marceau is speaking here of the use of mime within dance, and what he says about it is accurate. It is like a deaf-mute language. Unfortunately, this is quite often the means of communication chosen by those who would have dance tell a story. Reliance on mime is by no means limited to theatrical performances but is found as well among performances of folk and traditional dance. Balanchine, one of the greatest of contemporary classical choreographers, as Marceau indicates, is not among those choreographers who use dance as narrative. For Balanchine the capacities of dance to convey a story are limited. One can dance a love story, for example, in a pas de deux, but a complicated story is impossible. In any case, as far as Balanchine is concerned, there are more effective means of communicating plots and stories and the dance should instead develop its own special qualities.

These statements still do not offer explanations of the actual ways in which dance and language differ. Two scholars, Selma Jeanne Cohen and Jack Anderson, focus on one of the unique properties of dance, the kinesthetic, and by so doing begin to approach the question of differences. Cohen distinguishes between language and dance by distinguishing between concepts that are grasped by means of words and percepts that are grasped by means of the senses (in Nadel and Nadel, 1974:5). The strength of dance is that it deals in terms of percepts. Similarly, Anderson stresses the kinesthetic qualities of dance but goes further to suggest that these properties evoke sympathetic responses in the viewers. This power to evoke a kinesthetic response on the part of an audience is, in fact, the way in which dance communicates, whether the particular dance is telling a story, preaching a message, or simply conjuring a mood (Anderson, 1974:9).

What Anderson says about dance being a kinesthetic art is one crucial difference between dance and the other performing arts. It is important to recognize, however, that dance may convey meaning through other channels as well, and may convey it at different levels. Richard Waterman, in an article on the role of dance in human society, stresses that all dance patterns have meaning whether they are codified, named, and assigned denotative meaning, as in Indonesian dancing or in the more complex Hindu classical style, or whether they communicate in a less-structured and more direct way, sending affective messages by means of bodily movement that arouse an empathetic response in the viewer. It is the establishment of emphatic subliminal communication that dance does better than any other human social activity (1962:49-50).

Waterman sees dance as having the capacity to convey meaning in two different ways, one that we may call denotative and the other that we may call emphatic subliminal communication. This is a helpful distinction and does reflect some of the realities of the situation. However, it leaves out a whole body of dance behavior that falls somewhere in between denotative styles and those styles which convey meaning only subliminally. An example will indicate the complexities involved. Gloria Strauss, in a monograph on the art of the sleeve in Chinese dance (1975), compared Chinese sleeve gestures, or *hsiu*, with classical Indian *mudras*. Both might be called denotative systems, but the ways they convey information and the kinds of information they can convey vary greatly. *Mudras*, Strauss says, can relate an entire narrative. The *shui hsiu*, on the other hand, act as an addition or accompaniment to verbal exchanges, songs, and other body movements. The vocabularies of the two systems differ, therefore. The *shui hsiu* contain primarily gestures that act as verbs or modifiers, directing people or indicating how they feel. There are few, if any, gestures that act as nouns. The *mudra* vocabulary, in contrast, contains many gestures for nouns (rivers, flowers, snakes, and others) as well as many that act as verbs or modifiers (1975:38). In the one case, the gesture vocabulary is complete enough in itself to narrate a story. In the other case, the sleeve gestures only embroider the narrative.

Two categories proposed by Hanna are perhaps more in accord with actual dance behavior. She sees two dimensions to the socio-psychological functions of dance, the cognitive and

195

the affective (Hanna, 1975:10). The former refers to the fact that dance communicates some kind of information, and, like "other cultural codes and patterned interactions, dance is a way of ordering and categorizing experience" (ibid.:10). The affective function, in contrast, "is to provide a qualitative experience, a presence, immediacy, and envelopment of sensuousness (ibid.:11). There is no one-to-one correspondence between Waterman's denotative function and Hanna's cognitive one, but there is much similarity between the former's emphatic subliminal communication and the latter's affective function.

Underlying the whole issue of the communicative potential of dance is the larger question of what it is about dance that makes people choose it in certain instances and for certain purposes rather than some other medium of expression. Given a concern with this basic issue, then, anthropologists of dance should explore two areas: expression and content, two of the fundamental concepts in linguistics and allied disciplines. Two questions that must be examined in the area of expression in order for us to make any progress toward answering our larger questions are the following: 1) What *are* the channels through which communication takes place in the dance? 2) How does the structure of expression used by dance differ from that of language and of other systems of communication? Turning to the area of content, I see three significant problem areas: 1) dance types with respect to meaning, that is, mimetic, abstract, and metaphorical dances, 2) the significance of context in determining meaning, 3) intentional versus nonintentional meaning.

Because the meaning of dance is a subject treated only impressionistically in the past, most systematic investigation remains to be done.[9] My purpose here is to review what research of the past we may turn to our advantage in future studies, and to point out the various directions we might profitably go.

We may define expression in a variety of ways. Most simply, expression refers to the means by which content is expressed. We may also regard it as the medium of transmission, as does Sebeok:

Contact among emitters and receivers is established and maintained by miscellaneous flow-processes that link them across space and time, and our classification of sign systems becomes still further refined as this operationally crucial third factor—the medium of transmission—is taken into account (1974:234).

We have spoken about expression implicitly in discussing structural analysis and the patterning of units in dance, so let us now take up the question of channels of expression.

In many of the debates about the "meaning" aspect of dance, we are confronted by the question of by what means dance "communicates". Recall, for example, Anderson's statement that dance is not simply a visual art but a kinesthetic one as well which appeals to an inherent sense of motion. Hanna speaks more explicitly about the various channels used in the dance, referring to the dance as a multidimensional phenomenon directed toward the sensory modalities (1975:10).

What is immediately apparent is that dance is characterized by what one may call a multi-channel expression. Like language, its basic instrument is the human body. The human body moving in time and space utilizes channels we may designate as kinesthetic. It would not be exaggeration to suggest that this kinesthetic activity generates kinesthetic responses in the viewer although they generally are more restrained and less conscious than those of the performer. The phenomenon of toe tapping or the expression "caught up in the dance," as well as that of audiences falling into trance in response to watching dancers exhibiting trance behavior, testify to the empathy between performer and audience and to the existence of some kind of kinesthetic message being transmitted. Dance alone of the arts relies on the kinesthetic aspect of expression for much of its impact. Mime, too, has this aspect, but the object of mime is always to communicate some feeling, emotion, or story. In other words, movement in mime is always secondary to whatever is being communicated, whereas in dance movement is often an end in itself.

In addition to communication at the level of movement itself, the expressive structure of dance uses a number of other channels which, unlike the one mentioned above, it shares with other media. It is perhaps wisest to discuss the other channels in order of their importance. After the kinesthetic channel, the most significant channel in dance for transmitting information is the visual one. It is after all, the human body making patterns in space, which is characteristic of dance. There is great variety in conditions of visibility under which dance is viewed. Frequently, the dance is nothing more than a reflection of shadowy silhouettes projected by the smoke and flickering light of a campfire or images in a dimly lit church. At times, half of the population is forbidden to watch, although they may listen, as when ceremonies are held that women are not allowed to watch or when the uninitiated may not view ceremonies for initiated members of a society. Other dance performances take place outside during the day, where the only obstacles to visibility are other spectators, or else they are given in a theater illuminated by stage lights.

Dance sends signals by means of sound as well. I do not mean solely the sound that is a deliberate accompaniment to dance—while there are dances that have no musical accompaniment (for example, the silent women's dances of Yugoslavia), most dance is performed to some kind of musical background—but rather, the sounds of physical exertion: feet against ground or stage, breathing of people engaged in strenuous activity, rustle of costumes. As an example of the communicative potential of the sounds of breathing, I turn to the writing of Daniel Stern (*Mes Souvenirs,* 1806-1833) cited in Beaumont (1934). Stern is describing the dance master, Monsieur Abraham, and says of him, "Even his breathing was ageless and seemed like the rest of his person, to be subject to that lofty decorum of which he constituted himself the representative" (22).

Sometimes sounds accompanying exertion in dance are an integral part of the dance itself, for example, the sound of the heel work, or *zapateados,* in flamenco dance and in Mexican *huapangos,* the slapping of the bare foot on the floor in some of

198

the classical Indian dances, or the toe-heel beating the floor of the tap dancer. Without the sound dimension, none of these forms would be complete.

Still another channel in the expression structure of dance is that of touch. Even though this channel has been attenuated in many performance situations where performers and spectators are separated spatially, it has been, and still is, extremely important in many other dance situations. Especially striking is the use of touch in trance dance events around the world as a way of communicating a sense of contact with the phenomenal world. This usually occurs in situations that take the person out of the normal patterns of contact and which, therefore, are potentially dangerous. This is equally true of Balinese, Haitian, Bushman, and Pentecostal trance behavior. It may indeed be universal.

Touching also may be acceptable or encouraged in the dance context, while it is not allowed in nondance situations. In Western civilization, legitimate opportunities for contact between people of the opposite sex used to be rare. Dancing provided one of the most frequent occasions for tactile interaction, and people of both sexes put these opportunities to good advantage to size up potential marriage prospects. Poor health and other undesirable qualities were difficult to conceal in situations as intimate as the waltz or as physically taxing as a long night of country dances. Now that such opportunities abound, it appears that the closed couple dance has given way to the open, where partners are separated by a foot or more of floor space, or to dances where touching has become so ritualized that it communicates at the level of symbols, if at all, rather than at any tactile level. The kinds of touching in the line dances found throughout Eastern Europe and in Greece convey a sense of camaraderie, unity, and strength. Consider, for example, the Greek *hasapikos,* whose line of men with arms linked across the shoulders exudes solidarity, strength, and virility.

Something of a contrast to this is the circle of dancers huddled close to one another that typified the ghost dance of the

North American Indians. Here closeness of the dancers conveys their unity and the security that they find in their proximity to each other.

Last, dance involves the channel of smell, those odors characteristic of people involved in the physical activity of dancing. Just as the smell of a cockfight is distinctive and essential to the definition of that event, so are the odors of dancing essential to the total message of many dance events. The sense of smell, as well as that of touch, was important to the task of checking the physical fitness of a prospective mate. Unpleasant odors could indicate poor health and could render the candidate undesirable, if not unfit. Again, the situation where performers and spectators are physically separated presents an exception.

It is clear that dance utilizes a number of channels, the kinesthetic, which is crucial to it alone of all the arts, and the visual, aural, tactile, and olfactory. Given the number and variety of channels, the potential for communication is quite strong. If all the channels are transmitting the same message, then the impact is multiplied by a factor of five. It is perhaps this capacity to assault all of one's senses simultaneously that makes dance such a potent, often threatening, vehicle of expression. Ambiguity and the transmission of conflicting messages are also possible in view of the multi-channel nature of dance expression. In other words, you may be presented visually with one message while you are hearing or subliminally experiencing yet another. Ambiguity may be intentional or it may result from lack of shared knowledge between performers and spectators.

A line of inquiry that might elucidate the structure of expression in the dance would compare the impact of a live dance on an audience to the impact of a filmed performance. The nature of film eliminates essentially all but one channel, the visual one. You hear the accompanying music but not all the other sounds of a live performance. It would be enlightening to see what happens to the effectiveness of dance when its multi-channel nature is reduced to a single channel.

Having determined the channels through which communication occurs in dance, we may then go on to the second question in the area of expression. How does the structure of expression used by dance differ from that used by other systems of communication? This is a relatively straightforward problem involving the comparison of dance expression with other systems. The best and most obvious place to begin would be by comparing dance to language. First, we know what the structure of language is, so we may proceed directly to comparison instead of having first to do for language what we have done for dance. Second, the analogy between spoken language and the language of dance has become a commonplace in the literature without the kind of comparison I am suggesting ever having been made. This has resulted in our continually making assumptions about dance that may have no basis in fact because we are assuming that dance functions in the same manner as language. Our structural analyses are a good example of this. The search for levels comparable to phonemic, morphemic, lexemic, and syntactical is taken as a given. It may be, in fact, that we are distorting the phenomenon of dance by forcing it into a taxonomic system designed for a qualitatively different kind of phenomenon. This type of comparison may ultimately tell us that we have to deal with dance on its own terms. Having made the comparison, however, we will have gained the knowledge of which analogies we may profitably keep and which ones we must discard. Even if the comparison leads to negative results, in that there may be no useful analogies, we will have learned something about dance and other communicative systems by learning what it and they are not.

The comparison of dance expression to language expression is necessary because we have borrowed methods and theories for dance study from language. Once this is done, however, the logical next step is to proceed to comparing dance with those other forms of expressive behavior with communicative capabilities that are closest in form of expression to dance. Which are they? I have already mentioned the similarity between dance and mime, both of which use kinesthetic and visual

201

channels. The similarity is not so strong as it might be, however, because the ultimate purpose of mime is always to communicate a message, whereas this is not necessarily true of dance.

Another area that may well prove to be the most fruitful for comparative purposes is that of the theater. Like dance, theater is composed of multi-channel expressive behavior using visual, aural, tactile, and kinesthetic channels, although the last, in the case of the theater, is usually not the primary communicative channel. Theater has certainly a wealth of documentation, and, unlike most writing on dance, writers on the communicative aspects of the theater have often gone beyond mere impressionistic statements. Perhaps most relevant to our proposed comparison is Artaud, with his work on liberating theater from its role as a mere vehicle for the written or spoken word, when it should stand as a communicative system in its own right. The following statement by Artaud in his *The Theater and Its Double* illustrates his concern quite clearly:

> . . . the question of the theatre ought to arouse general attention, the implication being that theatre, through its physical aspect, since it requires expression in space (the only real expression, in fact) allows the magical means of art and speech to be exercised organically and altogether, like renewed exorcisms. The upshot of all this is that theatre will not be given its specific powers of action until it is given its language. That is to say: instead of continuing to rely upon texts considered definitive and sacred, it is essential to put an end to the subjugation of the theatre to the text, and to recover the notation of a kind of unique language half-way between gesture and thought (1958:89).

Artaud has defined a quality crucial to the distinction between many types of expressive behavior, that is, those behaviors which essentially take place in space and those which take place in time. Among the former would be the visual arts of painting and sculpture, dance, mime, the theater as Artaud would have it, and to some extent opera. The latter includes music, song, the genres of literature, and again dance, opera,

202

and theater. Expanding on this basic distinction, we can designate certain behaviors characterized by mode of presentation which is ordered in a linear fashion. They correspond quite closely to behaviors we have already designated as taking place in time. "Linear" refers to the fact that information is presented to us sequentially. We must take the information in the order in which it is presented in order for it to make sense; in other words, the ordering is crucial for the comprehension of the form, and this is as true of music as it is of literature. Given this and given also the fact that we can absorb only so much information in any given period of time, then we are limited as to the amount and kind of information we can convey by means of these sequential forms. For example, it has been suggested that while you have musical forms that are extremely complex rhythmically, and forms that are equally complex melodically, you almost never have forms that demonstrate both rhythmical and melodic complexity simultaneously. We simply could not process the information being communicated.

Nonlinear forms of expression, on the other hand, do not depend for comprehension on a sequential presentation of information. You may absorb the content of a painting or a sculpture at your leisure and in any order. Obviously, there are forms of expression that fall somewhere between the two extremes. They include theater as it is commonly defined, opera, and dance. The first two utilize more linear elements than the last; the first because it is still usually interpretation of a text, and the second because it interprets both a text and a musical text. At the same time, however, as Artaud has pointed out for the theater, both forms take place in space, and, more than simply filling space, they use space creatively and dramatically. It is because of this utilization of both time and space that theater and opera communicate differently and different things than do those arts that are linear. Dance is freer than theater or opera from linearity. Of necessity, dance is bound in time; dances have beginnings and ends, unlike paintings. But time for dance is simply a constant brought about by the physi-

203

cal fact of the body moving and making patterns in space. The essence of dance derives from the patterns it makes in space, not those it makes in time. Furthermore, dance can be comprehended without reference to sequential ordering of elements. Because dance is redundant, one has more than one opportunity to see any given segment. Each time the segment is repeated, the opportunity is there for different information to be derived from it or for the same information to be derived differently. Although it shares many of the channels with other arts, the impact of dance is distinctive because it, of all the performing arts, is free from most of the constraints of linearity.

Our discussion of the nature of expression in dance has given somewhat more precision to our metaphorical and impressionistic analogy between dance and language. It has, moreover, indicated areas that need further research. Let us now turn to the area of content to see if we may come closer still to answering our initial question: Why and when do people choose dance rather than some other medium of expression?

If one looks at dance around the world, it is apparent that three types of dance can be distinguished with regard to meaning: mimetic, abstract, and metaphorical. Curt Sachs applied slightly different terms to the categories:

> The image dance and the imageless dance are thus clearly distinguished one from another. If the forms and the movements stood in close relation to the theme and yet did not really describe the event itself, if they generalized and replaced it with a related event, then beside the mimetic and imageless dance, we might speak of an allegorical or a metaphorical dance. An initiation dance would be allegorical which has as its theme the flogging of the novice to promote power. A sex dance would be allegorical in which the men stamp on the ground, while the women respond to each stamp with an outcry. A marriage dance with the characteristics of a weapon dance would be allegorical (1937:57-58).

Though for purposes of discussion the three categories of

204

dance listed above will be used as if they described three clearly distinctive groups of dance phenomena, the truth is that dance phenomena are elusive and often difficult to assign to any one of the categories. Rather, they range themselves along a continuum, where it becomes a formidable task to draw the boundaries between them. As an example, let us take the first category, mimetic dance. One common form of mimetic dance is animal mime. Some animal mimes are uncanny in their imitation of real animals like the Yaqui deer dance and the Australian kangaroo dance. But there are animal mimes that bear only slight resemblence to their animal counterparts, like the California Pomo Indian prairie chicken dance, where the communication of the idea of a prairie chicken depends on shared understanding of the tradition, a headdress reminiscent of a prairie chicken tail, and dance gestures of the head vaguely suggestive of the motions of a bird.

Another kind of dance that often has mimetic qualities is the war dance. But this category brings up yet another problem for those who would make classifications. It is, for example, tempting to say that all animal mime dances and all war dances are mimetic. In fact, as we have seen above, many animal mimes are really metaphorical, and war dances are found in all three of our categories. At one extreme are those war dances such as the Morris-based dances which enact mock battles between opposing lines of dancers; and, at the other extreme are those which are simply circle dances, where the dancers recount the war deeds of ancestors.

Yet another difficulty is present in dance traditions that have retained their mimetic components long after those components have ceased to refer to any actually existing behaviors or ideas. This is a frequent occurrence in the formal aspect of the so-called classic traditions, like those of India and Bali. The informal, or recreational, dances tend to change all the time in response to events in the contemporary social scene. The formal tradition, however, is often very slow to change and is unresponsive to changes in the social setting. The result is that the formal dance eventually comes to have little or no relevance to the society that supports it. At this point several things may happen; the audience may be reeducated, a difficult process which Kapila Vatsyayan has documented for classical Indian dance; the dance may be changed to bring it into conformity with the contemporary setting; or the people may simply refuse to support it any longer and it will disappear, as nearly happened to some of the Balinese classical forms before the trend toward preserving traditions intact and the interest of tourists saved them.

An interesting line of inquiry might ask whether mimetic dance forms have a longer or shorter life span than do abstract or metaphorical forms. What may, in fact, happen is that mimetic dances that are no longer culturally meaningful may be retained in the repertoire but enjoyed as abstract dances, that is, simply for the movements themselves. Much of the gesture language of classical ballet, for example, conveys little to contemporary audiences, yet those ballets which incorporate this language of gesture are performed and enjoyed for the sake of movement. When older styles of mime are so conspicuous as to detract from the movement itself, then the ballets which use them tend to disappear unless one keeps them as sentimental reminders of the old days or views them as comedies. In light of this, Michael Fokine was undoubtedly wise to reject the traditional Russian pantomime in favor of a somewhat more subtle approach in his ballet "Scheherazade":

> In Scheherazade, when the Shah was battling with himself whether to kill Zobëida along with all the other wives, his vengeful brother did not embark on a long spiel such as: Listen (hand extended to the Shah). Just think (tapping his forehead) that your queen (pointing at Zobëida, then sketching a crown over his own head) was making love (cuddling his own body with both arms) to a Negro (making a fierce grimace and passing his hand like a shade down in front of his face to convey darkness). No, the King of Persia, hand on sword-hilt, paced very slowly across the front of the stage and with one foot turned the Negro's body over, so that he lay face upwards (Buckle, 1971:142-143).

The Meaning of Dance

Abstract dances, that is, dances in which the movement of the body itself is the focal point, seem to occur as frequently and to be as old as both mimetic and metaphorical dances.

Metaphorical dance, our third type, occupies a position midway between the abstract and the mimetic, and, like the two others, never seems to occur as the only form of dance in any society. The properties of this type of dance are illustrated by rain dances of the Sioux and the Monumbo Papua of New Guinea. The Sioux place a vessel of water on the ground, dance around it four times, throw themselves on the ground, and then drink up the water. The New Guinea group bring rain by having two masked dancers dance around a container of water, after which the women of the tribe gather around the container and drink the water. These two dances, in combining circling, abstract dance with symbols of water and rain and the associated pantomime, are midway between two other rain dances. The northwestern Australian tribes bring rain in an abstract dance circling around a magic stone. The Arunta, also of Australia, perform an imitative fan dance that causes the wind to blow, bringing rain (Sachs, 1937:114).

Although Sachs's type of explanation is no longer fashionable, he has brought out a problem area worthy of investigation, particularly if we are concerned with the communicative aspects of dance. He correctly delineated three kinds of dance I have called abstract, mimetic, and metaphorical. If, as we know, the dance repertoire of most cultures includes or has included in the past all three types, then we may assume that each type differs from the others in its communicative nature. Were it otherwise, we must assume some kind of redundance that would be unusual. What then becomes significant is .the worldwide geographic distribution of the three types, their distribution throughout history, and their distribution through time and by occasion within individual societies.

The first kind of survey should give us a map of world dance in terms of the three types, which we can then match with maps of other traits. This procedure is similar to what Lomax has attempted in his choreometrics project, where he was concerned with matching gross movement styles with subsistence patterns and movement styles in everyday life. The second, an historical survey, should give us insight into changes which, in turn, may be correlated with other preferences. We have already briefly surveyed the classical ballet in these terms and have seen the swing back and forth between *ballet à entrée* and *ballet d'action*. Perhaps it may be that the changes come about simply as a result of the desire for something new. In other cases the change may occur as a result of pressures or influences from the outside, as I suspect is the case with the Hawaiian dance (see Kealiinohomoku, 1973). The last type of investigation is, in reality, the first, since it is only from the survey of individual societies that we can go on to more general types of surveys.

This brings us to the second question under the broad heading of content: What, if any, is the significance of context in determining meaning in the dance?

> It should be noted that the relationship between context and meaning is crucial as far as a language is concerned since the same word may have a variety of meanings depending upon the context. Metaphorical language and figures of speech result from this capacity (Sebeok, 1974:243).

If we want to learn how and what dance communicates, then this is a question that must concern us. First of all, context has two different meanings of relevance for the dance. In the narrower sense it refers to the context of individual steps and combinations of steps within the totality called a dance. In the broader sense we may use it to refer to the context within which the totality "dance" takes place. To avoid confusion, I shall use the terms "context" for the narrow sense and "occasion" for the broader sense.

There are many interesting examples of the relationship between meaning and context in the classic ballet. It is a frequent occurrence that the same steps, mime gestures, or short combinations are repeated in very different contexts throughout a ballet. Take, for example, "Swan Lake"; the lyrical, swan-like movements of Odette in the first act are imitated by Odile in the third act in order to convince the prince that the two women are, in fact, the same. The movements performed by Odette convey a fragile, vulnerable quality, while the same movements done by Odile take on an unnerving, sinister quality. We can turn to "Giselle" for another example. The *ballottés* and *grands jetés* which constitute the first-act pas de deux between Albrecht and Giselle are repeated in the mad scene that follows Giselle's learning that Albrecht is betrothed to another. In the first case they convey the lightheartedness and joy of love; in the second they stand as a tragic reminder of that same love now lost. Another example can be drawn from the sleeve miming in the classic Chinese opera. The standard gesture for helplessness, *chih hsiu*, if performed while the actor is singing, means that the song is about to end, rather than conveying helplessness (Strauss, 1975:36-37).

Meaning seems to change with occasion as well. We have referred previously to the Haitian example where whole choreographies or dances are perceived as being different phenomena in different situations. The same choreography done in a voodoo ceremony will be referred to as "religion"; when it is performed in a cabaret, it will be called "dance." Other obvious changes in meaning occur when dances are removed from their original setting to be performed as theater pieces.

The third question to be considered in our discussion of content is that which treats intentional versus unintentional meaning of dance. This, I think, is a problem as significant for dance as it is for language. It involves the whole area of interpretation on the part of both the dancer and the spectator. The frequent charge that dancing is immoral can result from a mismatch between the performer's intended meaning and that held by the spectators. A good example is the attitude described by Monica Wilson for African dance during the colonial situation:

The girls' initiation dance and the boys' circumcision dance of the Xhosa were actually prohibited by law in the Ciskei, as being "contrary to good morals," and the quivering of the muscles which played a major part in the ordinary dances of the young people was forbidden to Christians at least in some communions (Hunter, 1936, p.375). For their part, many Nguni regarded western ballroom dancing in which partners held one another as highly indecent, and indeed one independent African state in which people of Nguni origin wield power, Malawi, has prohibited it (Wilson *in* La Fontaine, 1972:194).

A similar misunderstanding occurred in the colonial American South when blacks were converted to various Christian denominations, many of which frowned on dancing. The sin of dancing was avoided and the benefits of dancing retained by dancers imposing certain restrictions on movement. Crossing the feet and lifting the feet from the floor were among the banned movements (see Emery, 1972:122).

An analysis of the different meanings or interpretations possible in the performances of La Argentina, one of the most famous of Spanish dancers, illustrates another kind of ambiquity:

> Her glorious smile was the symbol to people of a sunny, carefree Spain. . . . In Argentina's case people mistook her personality for representationalism. She was Spain. Because she danced few regional dances, her gesture had the grace of a diplomatic mission and she could be at ease in London, Paris, or New York. Hers was the universal symbol; she was a lady, and a commercial triumph. Her wardrobe symbolized Paris; her dancing, the gardens of Spain; her bows, the envy of any Russian ballerina; and her gentility, that of an English lady. Argentina offended no one who could afford the price of a ticket. Argentina's dancing, therefore, was the genteel aristocratic symbol of a wilting social order. . . . She was the essence of Spain if you could afford it (Maracci *in* Sorell, 1951:162-63).

As Maracci has indicated, there are many possible interpretations of La Argentina and her dancing, and the relationship of

210

all or any of them to interpretations intended by Argentina is problematical. Wilson has considered this difficulty, though from a slightly different perspective:

> When people of different languages and cultures interact, failures of communication are legion, and are perhaps most numerous when they involve symbols of which the users are only half-conscious. Furthermore, strangers sometimes suppose content that does not exist (*in* La Fontaine, 1972:197).

What the examples I have given and the statements I have cited all indicate is that in dance, as in other media of communication, there is ever present the potential for ambiguity of meaning resulting from the noncommunication of an intended meaning and the communication or reception of a meaning that has not been intended. It has also been observed, however, that dance, more frequently than other forms of expression, is often the source of contradictory messages. A partial explanation of this takes us back to our discussion of dance expression. As we noted then, dance expression takes place via a number of channels at the same time, so that potential for communication is five times greater than in a form that uses only one channel. Potential for confusion, whether deliberate or unintentional, is also five times greater. What this means is that any discussion of meaning in a dance form or a specific performance must consider all the possible meanings from the point of view of both performer and spectator.

In exploring the possibilities of the potential for communication in dance, we have tried to move beyond the realm of impressionistic statements and point to specific areas of investigation for which we have both the tools and the data. By systematically considering expression and content in the dance, we will make considerable progress toward answering the larger question about dance which has always been there implicitly serving as inspiration for research in dance from the anthropological perspective; namely, what is it about dance that prompts people to choose it in specific instances and for specific purposes rather than some other medium of communication.

❧ 10 ❧

CONCLUSIONS

AS AN ANTHROPOLOGIST concerned with human behavior, I have spoken about the integration of individuals and culture, and, correspondingly, of the impossibility of wrenching dance out of its proper context as an aspect of human behavior. As an anthropologist concerned specifically with the dance, I recognize the necessity of isolating the focus of concern for the purpose of understanding certain aspects of it, most often the formal ones. The study of dance is not unique in having both formal and contextual aspects, although its nature may render it more susceptible to dual concerns. It is an area, for example, that has a vast literature produced by scholars other than anthropologists who have discussed primarily its form. This is not true of other aspects of human behavior, such as kinship, which have been the domain exclusively of anthropologists. Anthropologists investigating kinship have analyzed both the forms it takes and its meaning within the cultural context.

We may learn something about the nature of the subdiscipline by comparing the European tradition of dance study with that developed in America. In America most studies of the dances of American Indians were done by anthropologists, who were concerned with preserving as much as possible about societies and cultures they felt were rapidly disappearing. In the process they collected information on the dance traditions. The information about dance is overwhelmingly in the area of context rather than form, so that we have data about dance societies, dancers, and the role of dance within the culture but almost no data about the actual choreography of the dances, with the exception of floor plan. When American anthropologists turned their attention to peoples other than American Indians, they tended toward the same kind of data collection with regard to dance.

Europe, in contrast, had a long tradition of dance study by folklorists and dance scholars. For the most part these people focused their attention on the folk or peasant dance traditions found all over Europe. With few exceptions (the Jankovič sisters for Yugoslav dance and Geörgy Martin for Hungarian dance), the emphasis was on the form of the dance rather than its context.

The explanation for the emphasis on context, in the American case, and on form, in the European case, is a relatively simple one. Anthropologists who did the collecting in the United States regarded dance as only one aspect among many in a culture, and most often dance was accorded less importance than many other cultural and social institutions like kinship, house types, and religion. Moreover, anthropologists had developed the tools and techniques for recording information on the latter kinds of traits and institutions, while techniques for recording dance were virtually nonexistent.

European folklorists and dance scholars, on the other hand, were interested in the dance as a phenomenon unto itself rather than as an aspect of human behavior integrated into a cultural context. Many of them had also had dance training so that they could learn the dances and reproduce them at their convenience. Even more important, they had the tools for recording dance. Workable notation systems for dance had been devised and put to use much earlier in Europe than in the

213

United States. Much of the mystery that makes dance such a frightening human artifact to describe disappears when one is working in a long-standing tradition of recording systems.

We are not doomed to endless repetition of this long history of either form or context. Without abandoning the anthropological perspective, we may legitimately focus on both the formal aspects of dance and the larger context in which they are embedded. We do forsake the task of anthropology, however, when we concern ourselves with form alone, letting that concern stand as an end in itself. Analysis of form is a means to an end. It is no more than this, and by itself it can be nothing other than an intellectual exercise. Anthropologists treat the phenomenon of human behavior, not merely the pieces of that phenomenon. We dissect the phenomenon to find out what makes it tick. It is tempting to stop there, anesthetized by the sheer intellectual pleasure of dissection. To reach any understanding about human beings and the world they create, however, we must put the products of analysis back together so that the final synthesis tells us something more about the phenomenon than the structure of its individual parts.

Throughout the book we have looked at dance both analytically and synthetically. In the process it has become clear that the anthropology of dance is something more than any of its parts. Dance viewed from the anthropological perspective is inextricably bound up with individuals and culture in a mutually affecting relationship. Anthropology, in turn, gains insight into human motivations and behavior by its association with an aspect of human behavior that may well be unique in terms of its statements about people.

One reason for the inseparability of dance and culture, except for analytical purposes, is the inseparability of dance from its creator and instrument of expression. The creators and instruments live in a cultural context that shapes them and their dance. Dance does not exist apart from dancers. We must, therefore, not only look at the form of dance but consider as well the meanings it has for the people who create it, do it, and watch it.

The relationship of dance to culture is by no means a simple one. The early studies of dance by anthropologists, unlike recent ones, did posit a simple, direct relationship. Simple societies had simple dances. Moreover, because dancing was regarded as being a primitive response, the early evolutionists contended that it had greater meaning for primitive peoples and would be abandoned with the coming of civilization. Studies of cultures and societies as integrated wholes brought with them a more realistic attitude toward the role of dance within human society. They did not regard simplicity or complexity of dance form as a function of the level of a society or culture, and they saw dance as having many different functions, depending on the cultural context of which it was an integrated part. Studies of change were even more committed to understanding the complex relationship between dance and culture, since neither changes in the form nor changes in the meaning of dance can be understood without reference to the cultural context. Form and meaning, moreover, may change at different rates. Finally, change may occur in response to changes in the larger setting or it may occur when the setting is relatively stable.

One of the recent approaches in the anthropology of dance deals with the symbolic aspects of dance. Traditionally, symbolism has been an area that has been concerned almost exclusively with form. This is true of dance symbolism as well as symbolism in other realms. If we contend that the dance form is inseparable from the dancer, who is inseparable from context, then an equally important set of questions must be asked about the reasons for calling that particular kind of symbolism into play. When and why do people feel it necessary to identify themselves through certain symbols in the dance? How is it that they may use one set of symbols on one occasion and another

215

on a second occasion? Of interest as well, admittedly, are the symbols themselves and how they have come to be selected. But even here context cannot be ignored for long because symbols do not appear in a vacuum; they appear in response to rivals and opposition more often than not, and they frequently are symbols borrowed from opposing groups.

In the most recent developments in the anthropology of dance, which I regard as heralding two major future directions, we may see the most sophisticated treatment to date of the relationship between dance form and dance meaning and between dance and culture. In the context of dance research past and present the two large categories into which new studies may be placed represent opposite processes. Studies of aesthetics and creativity have their basis in structural analyses of dance form, and only very recently have we begun to go beyond the analysis of form to consider how it shapes and is shaped by cultural standards and values relating to dance. Intimately related to these standards of appropriate form is, of course, the idea of creativity. The creative dancer or choreographer must be aware of the limits to which aesthetic principles may be stretched or changed. No meaningful statements about either aesthetics or creativity can be made without reference to both form and context.

The second category of dance research, that concerned with the meaning of dance, has had, in contrast to the category of aesthetics and creativity, a long history of focusing almost exclusively on the contextual level and ignoring form. The result has been impressionistic statements about the communicative powers of dance. Only recently have we stopped to consider the implications of either the form of dance or the form of communicative channels in general. That we are working toward a synthesis of form and context in the areas of aesthetics, creativity, and communication indicates, I think, a clearer appreciation of the complexity of that synthesis than has characterized any past era in the anthropology of dance.

In a field as young as the anthropology of dance, we cannot

sit back, contemplate the rise and fall of various schools of thought and theoretical approaches, and make any definitive statements about the nature of the field. At this point, we can only engage in a kind of taking stock. It is appropriate that we should look at where we have been, where we are, and where we might be going in the development of the field. A luxury we cannot afford, however, is to rest on our accomplishments to date, however important and tangible they might be.

If anthropology claims a lack of good descriptive studies, how much more lacking in that respect is the anthropology of dance. As the discussion of the comparative method in Chapter 6 demonstrated, the number of studies available for comparative purposes is extremely small. Now that our techniques for collecting data are more or less adequate to the task, we must apply them and ourselves to the end of filling this gap. Good description is ultimately the foundation for all else we might wish to do.

At the same time, we cannot afford to cease exploring the realm of theory. To do so would be to stop growing as a discipline, to fall back to the collection of data as an end in itself, and to produce endless and meticulous descriptions and analyses. In short, we would lose sight of our ultimate goal, which is to document dance as an aspect of human behavior.

One of the great strengths of the field of the anthropology of dance is that there are as many geographic areas and topical areas represented as there are people working in the field. Because it is a young field, there are relatively few "schools." This has encouraged innovative research characterized by an eclecticism of background that has generally contributed to the growth of the field. In addition, it is small enough so that one can speak of a community of scholars, aware of and drawing on each other's work, and benefiting from that kind of access and exchange of views. The field has grown beyond the stage where each new scholar essentially reinvents it in isolation, unaware of those few others with similar interests. Being trained as an anthropologist of the dance today is an actual possibility. There are courses covering different aspects of the field taught in many universities. There are collections of articles and source books which can be used as texts. One no longer has to spend all one's research time ferreting out articles in obscure journals and languages not readily accessible to most dance scholars. There is a national organization that facilitates the exchange of views through journals, newsletters, and national conferences. In December of 1976 a conference was held to discuss the format and content of a multi-volume encyclopedia of dance. The encyclopedia is now on its way to becoming a reality, and perspectives and techniques of the anthropology of dance will be featured in it. All of these developments mean that one can now acquire the basic knowledge of the field in a systematic, relatively economical fashion, which frees one to go beyond that basic core of knowledge and open new avenues of research.

In the past, individuals who devoted their research to the dance did so, for the most part, outside the established field of anthropology. While many produced studies that were, in fact, essentially anthropological, they did so without benefit of a systematic knowledge of that discipline. This serves as a partial explanation of why developments in dance research tended to lag behind the theoretical and methodological advances in the field of anthropology. We have arrived now at the point where many dance researchers are trained as anthropologists, first and foremost, with a specialty in the dance behavior of human beings. Two advantages result: first, we are not forced into the position of trying to keep up with advances in a field not our own, a situation where we can only lag behind; second, the process of integrating dance and culture is easier, since we must be equally concerned with both at all times.

Why should anthropology concern itself with the phenomenon of dance? Many years ago Sachs offered one answer:

If the dance, inherited from brutish ancestors, lives in all mankind as a necessary motor-rhythmic expression of excess energy

218

Conclusions

and of the joy of living, then it is only of slight importance for anthropologists and social historians. If it is established, however, that an inherited predisposition develops in many ways in the different groups of man and in its force and direction is related to other phenomena of civilization, the history of dance will then be of great importance for the study of mankind (1937:12).

Dance cannot meaningfully be divorced from culture, in other words, and that unity is properly the domain and the responsibility of anthropology.

REFERENCES CITED

Ablon, Joan. "Relocated American Indians in the San Francisco Bay Area: Social Interaction and Indian Identity." *Human Organization* 23 (1964), 296-304.

Anderson, Jack. *Dance.* New York: Newsweek Books, 1974.

Arbeau, Thoinot. *Orchesographie.* Lengres: Imprime par Jehan des Preyz, 1588.

Artaud, Antonin. *The Theater and Its Double.* Mary Caroline Richards, trans. New York: Grove Press, 1958.

Backman, E. Louis. *Religious Dances in the Christian Church and in Popular Medicine.* London: George Allen and Unwin, 1952.

Balch, Thomas Willing. *The Philadelphia Assemblies.* Philadelphia: Allen, Lane and Scott, 1916.

Beaumont, Cyril. *A Bibliography of Dancing.* London: The Dancing Times, 1929.

———. *A Miscellany for Dancers.* London: Beaumont, 1934.

Beckwith, Martha. "Dance Forms of the Moqui and Kwakiutl Indians." Proceedings of the 15th International Congress of Americanists (Quebec) 2 (1906-1907), 79-114.

Benedict, Ruth. *Patterns of Culture.* Boston: Houghton, 1934.

Bie, Oscar. *Der Tanz.* Berlin: J. Bard, 1919.

Birdwhistell, Ray. "Kinesics in the Context of Motor Habits." Paper read at the annual meeting of the American Anthropological Association, 1957.

Bittle, William E. "The Manatidie: A Focus for Kiowa Tribal Identity." *Plains Anthropologist* 7 (1962), 152-63.

Blacking, John A. *How Musical is Man?* Seattle: University of Washington Press, 1973.

Boas, Franziska. *The Function of Dance in Human Society.* New York: Dance Horizons, 1944.

Bonnet, Jacques. *Histoire générale de la Danse, Sacrée et Prophane.* Paris: Chez d'Houry, 1724.

Bourguignon, Erika. "Trance Dance." *Dance Perspectives* no. 35. 1968.

Buckle, Richard. *Nijinsky.* New York: Avon Books, 1971.

References Cited

Burnaby, Andrew. *Burnaby's Travels through North America*. New York: A. Wessels, 1904.

Cahusac, Louis de. *La Danse Ancienne et Moderne*. Paris: Chez La Haye, 1754.

Cohen, Selma Jeanne, ed. *Dance as a Theatre Art: Source Readings in Dance History from 1581 to the Present*. New York: Dodd, Mead, 1974.

Colby, Benjamin, and Pierre Van Den Berghe. *Ixil Country*. Berkeley: University of California Press, 1969.

Comstock, Tamara, ed. *New Dimensions in Dance Research: Anthropology and Dance* (The American Indian). New York: Committee on Research in Dance, 1974.

Covarrubias, Miguel. *Mexico South, the Isthmus of Tehuantepec*. New York: Knopf, 1946.

Cresswell, Nicholas. *The Journal of Nicholas Cresswell, 1774-1777*. New York: Dial Press, 1928.

D'Aronco, Gianfranco. *Storia della Danza Popolare e d'Arte*. Firenze: Casa Editrice Leo S. Olschki, 1962.

Dell, Cecily. *A Primer for Movement Description*. New York: Dance Notation Bureau, 1970.

Densmore, Frances. *Chippewa Music*. Bureau of American Ethnology Bulletin nos. 45, 53. 1913.

DeVos, George A., and Lola Romanucci-Ross, eds. *Ethnic Identity: Cultural Continuities and Change*. Palo Alto: Mayfield Publishing, 1975.

Earle, Alice Morse. *Colonial Dames and Good Wives*. New York: Frederick Ungar Publishing, 1962.

Edgerton, Robert B. *Methods and Styles in the Study of Culture*. San Francisco: Chandler and Sharp, 1974.

Emery, Lynne Fauley. *Black Dance in the United States from 1619 to 1970*. Palo Alto: National Press Books, 1972.

Emmerson, George S. *A Social History of Scottish Dance*. Montreal: McGill-Queen's University Press, 1972.

Evans-Pritchard, E.E. "The Dance." *Africa* 1:446-62, 1928.

Feuillet, Raoul. *Chorégraphie, ou L'Art de d'ecrire la Danse*. Paris: Feuillet, 1700.

Fithian, Philip Vickers. *Journal and Letters of Philip Vickers Fithian, 1773-1774: A Plantation Tutor of the Old Dominion*. H.D. Farish, ed. Williamsburg, Va.: Colonial Williamsburg, 1943.

Frake, Charles. "A Structural Description of Subanun 'Religious Behavior' " In *Explorations in Cultural Anthropology*. Ward Goodenough, ed. New York: McGraw-Hill, 1964.

Gamble, John J. "Forty-nine: a Modern Social Dance." *American Indian Hobbyist* 6 (1960), 86-88.

Garbett, G. Kingsley. "The Analysis of Social Situations." *Man* 5 (1970): 214-27.

221

References Cited

Goodenough, Ward. *Explorations in Cultural Anthropology*. New York: McGraw-Hill, 1974.

Grigoriev, S.L. *The Diaghilev Ballet 1909-1929*. Baltimore: Penguin Books, 1960.

Hall, Fernau. "Noh, Kabuki, Kathakali." *Sangeet Natak* 7 (1968): 33-75.

Hanna, Judith Lynne. "African Dance as Education." In *Impulse 1965: Dance and Education Now*. Marian Van Tuyl, ed. San Francisco: Impulse Publications, 1965.

————. "Review" [*African Art in Motion*], *Dance Research Journal* 7 (1974-75): 31-33.

————. "Toward a Cross-Cultural Conceptualization of Dance and Some Correlate Considerations." IX International Congress of Anthropological and Ethnological Sciences, Chicago, 1973 (rev. 1975).

Haskell, Arnold L. *Ballet Russe: the Age of Diaghilev*. London: Weidenfeld and Nicolson, 1968.

Hughes, Russell M. *Dance as an Art Form, Its History and Development*. New York: Barnes, 1933.

Hutchinson, Ann. *Labanotation*. New York: New Directions, 1954.

Kaeppler, Adrienne. "Preservation and Evolution of Form and Function in Two Types of Tongan Dance." In *Polynesian Culture History: Essays in Honor of Kenneth P. Emory*. Genevieve Highland, ed. Bernice P. Bishop Museum Special Publication 56 (1967a): 503-536.

————. "The Structure of Tongan Dance." Ph.D. diss., University of Hawaii, 1967b.

Kammen, Michael G. *People of Paradox: an Inquiry Concerning the Origins of American Civilization*. New York: Knopf, 1972.

Kealiinohomoku, Joann. "A Comparative Study of Dance as a Constellation of Motor Behaviors among African and United States Negroes." M.A. thesis, Northwestern University, 1965.

————. "Hopi and Polynesian Dance: a Study in Cross-Cultural Comparisons." *Ethnomusicology* 11 (1967): 343-57.

————. "Culture Change—Functional and Dysfunctional Expressions of Dance, a Form of Affective Culture." IX International Congress of Anthropological and Ethnological Sciences, Chicago, 1973.

————. "Dance Culture as a Microcosm of Holistic Culture." In *New Dimensions in Dance Research: Anthropology and Dance (The American Indian)*. Tamara Comstock, ed. New York: Committee on Research in Dance, 1974a: 99-106.

————. "Field Guides." In *New Dimensions in Dance Research: Anthropology and Dance (The American Indian)*. Tamara Comstock, ed. New York: Committee on Research in Dance, 1974b:245-60.

————. "Review Number One [Choreometrics] Caveat on Causes and Correlations." *CORD News* 6 (1974c: 20-24.

References Cited

Keil, Charles. *Urban Blues*. Chicago: University of Chicago Press, 1966.

Kelley, Jr., Joseph J. *Life and Times in Colonial Philadelphia*. Harrisburg, Penn.: Stackpole Books, 1973.

Kercheval, Samuel. *A History of the Valley of Virginia*. Woodstock, Va.: W.N. Grabill, 1902.

Khudekov, S.N. *Istoria Tantsev*. St. Petersburg, 1913.

Kinney, Troy, and M.W. Kinney. *The Dance: Its Place in Art and Life*. New York: Stokes, 1924.

Kirstein, Lincoln. *Dance: A Short History of Classical Theatrical Dancing*. New York: Putnam's 1935.

————. *The Classic Ballet*. New York: Knopf, 1952.

————. *Movement and Metaphor*—Four Centuries of Ballet. New York: Praeger, 1970.

Kroeber, Alfred L. *Style and Civilizations*. Berkeley: University of California Press, 1963.

Kurath, Gertrude Prokosch. "Dance: Folk and Primitive." In *Dictionary of Folklore, Mythology and Legend*, Maria Leach and J. Fried, eds., vol. 1, pp. 277-96. New York: Funk and Wagnalls, 1949.

————. "A Choreographic Questionnaire." *Midwest Folklore* 2 (1952): 53-55.

————. "Dance Relatives of Mid-Europe and Middle America." *Journal of American Folklore* 69 (1956): 286-98.

————. "Panorama of Dance Ethnology." *Current Anthropology* 1 (1960): 233-54.

————. "Research Methods and Background of Gertrude Kurath." In *New Dimensions in Dance Research: Anthropology and Dance (The American Indian)*. Tamara Comstock, ed. New York: Committee on Research in Dance, 1974, pp. 35-44.

Kurath, Gertrude Prokosch, and Samuel Martí. *Dances of Anáhuac: The Choreography for Music of Precortesian Dances*. Viking Fund Publications in Anthropology No. 38. New York: Wenner-Gren Foundation for Anthropological Research, 1964.

Laban, Juana de. "Introduction to Dance Notation." *Dance Index* 5 (1946): 89-126.

————. "Movement Notation: Its Significance to the Folklorist." *Journal of American Folklore* 67 (1954): 291-95.

Laban, Rudolf. *Principles of Dance and Movement Notation*. New York: Dance Horizons, 1956.

————. *The Mastery of Movement*. London: The Whitefriar's Press, 1960.

La Fontaine, J.S., ed. *The Interpretation of Ritual*. London: Tavistock Publications, 1972.

Lamb, Martha J., and Mrs. Burton Harrison. *History of the City of New York: Its Origin, Rise, and Progress*. Vol.1. New York: Barnes, 1877.

Land, Robert. "The First Williamsburg Theater." *William and Mary Quarterly* (series 3) 5 (1948): 359-74.

References Cited

Lawler, Lillian. *The Dance in Ancient Greece.* Seattle: University of Washington Press, 1964.

Leach, M. and J. Fried, eds. *Standard Dictionary of Folklore, Mythology and Legend.* New York: Funk and Wagnalls, 1949.

Lomax, Alan. *Folk Song Style and Culture.* Washington, D.C.: American Association for the Advancement of Science, Publication No. 88, 1968.

————. "Choreometrics and Ethnographic Filmmaking." *Filmmakers Newsletter* 4 (1971a): 22-30.

————. "Toward an Ethnographic Film Archive." *Filmmakers Newsletter* 4 (1971b): 31-38.

Louis, Maurice. *Le Folklore et la Danse.* Paris: G.P. Maisonneuve et Larose, 1963.

Malinowski, Bronislaw. *Argonauts of the Western Pacific.* London: Routledge, 1922.

Marceau, Marcel. "Interview with Marcel Marceau." *Dance Magazine* (August 1975a): 36.

————. *Souvenir Program.* New York: Dunetz and Lovett, 1975b.

Martin, György, and Ernö Pésovar. "A Structural Analysis of Hungarian Folk Dance." Acta Ethnografica Academiae Scientiarum Hungaricae 10 (1961).

Maugh, T.H. "Creativity: Can it be Detected? Can it be Taught?" *Science* 179 (1974): 1273

Mead, Margaret. *Coming of Age in Samoa.* New York: Morrow, 1928.

Mead, Margaret, and Ruth Bunzel, eds. *The Golden Age of Anthropology.* New York: George Braziller, 1960.

Merriam, Alan P. *The Anthropology of Music.* Evanston, Ill.: Northwestern University Press. 1964.

————. "Anthropology and the Dance." In *New Dimensions in Dance Research: Anthropology and Dance (The American Indian).* Tamara Comstock, ed. New York: Committee on Research in Dance, 1974, pp. 9-28.

Michaelis, Anthony R. *Research Films in Biology, Anthropology, Psychology, and Medicine.* New York: Academic Press, 1955.

Mitchell, J.C. "The Kalela Dance: Aspects of Social Relationships Among Urban Africans in Northern Rhodesia." Rhodes-Livingstone Papers No. 27, 1956.

Mooney, James. *The Ghost-dance Religion and the Sioux Outbreak of 1890.* Chicago: University of Chicago Press. 1965.

Morgan, Edmund S. *Virginians at Home.* New York: Holt, Rinehart and Winston, 1952.

Morgan, Lewis Henry. *League of the Ho-de-no-sau-nee, or Iroquois.* Rochester: Sage and Bros., 1850.

Nadel, Myron, and Constance Nadel, eds. *The Dance Experience: Readings in Dance Appreciation.* New York: Praeger, 1970.

References Cited

Narodny, Ivan. *The Dance*. New York: National Society of Music, 1917.

Palmer, R.R. *A History of the Modern World*. New York: Knopf, 1963.

Parsons, Talcott, and Edward A. Shils, eds. *Toward a General Theory of Action*. Cambridge: Harvard University Press, 1951.

Peacock, James L. *Rites of Modernization: Symbolic and Social Aspects of Indonesian Proletarian Drama*. Chicago: University of Chicago Press, 1968.

Powers, William K. "Round Dance." *Powwow Trails* 1 (1964): 5.

———. "Rabbit Dance." *Powwow Trails* 1 (1965): 6.

Radcliffe-Brown, A.R. *Structure and Function in Primitive Society*. New York: The Free Press, 1965.

Radin, Paul. *Primitive Religion: Its Nature and Origin*. New York: Dover Publications, 1957.

Ranger, T.O. *Dance and Society in Eastern Africa, 1890-1970*. Berkeley: University of California Press, 1975.

Richardson, Philip J.S. *The Social Dances of the Nineteenth Century in England*. London: Herbert Jenkins, 1960.

Royce, Anya Peterson. "Five Centuries of Dance Notation." Manuscript, 1975.

———. "Social and Political Aspects of Dance Behavior in Plural Societies." Manuscript, 1973.

———. "Choreology Today: a Review of the Field." In *New Dimensions in Dance Research: Anthropology and Dance (The American Indian)*. Tamara Comstock, ed. New York: Committee on Research in Dance, 1974, pp. 47-84.

———. *Prestigio y Afiliación en una Comunidad Urbana: Juchitán, Oaxaca*. Serie de Antropología Social #37. Mexico, D.F.: Instituto Nacional Indigenista, 1975.

Rust, Frances. *Dance in Society: an Analysis of the Relationship between the Social Dance and Society in England from the Middle Ages to the Present Day*. London: Routledge and Kegan Paul, 1969.

Sachs, Curt. *World History of the Dance*. New York: Norton, 1937.

Saint-Léon, Charles. *Stenochorégraphie*. Paris: St. Petersburg, 1852.

Saldaña, Nancy. "La Malinche: Her Representation in Dances of Mexico and the United States." Ethnomusicology 10 (1966): 298-309.

Schneider, Gretchen. "Pigeon Wings and Polkas: The Dance of the California Miners." *Dance Perspectives* 39, 1969.

Schoolcraft, H.R. *Personal Memoirs of a Resident of Thirty Years with the Indian Tribes*. Philadelphia: Lippincott, 1851.

Sebeok, Thomas. "Semiotics: a Survey of the State of the Art." In *Current Trends in Linquistics*. Vol. 12. T.A. Sebeok, ed. The Hague: Mouton, 1974.

Shay, Anthony V. "The Functions of Dance in Human Societies: An Approach Using Context (Dance Event) not Content (Movements and Gestures) for Treating Dance as Anthropological Data." M.A. thesis, California State College, Los Angeles, 1971.

References Cited

Shoup, Gail. "Present Trends in Dance Notation." M.A. thesis, University of California at Los Angeles, 1951.

Slotkin, J.S. "An Intertribal Dancing Contest." *Journal of American Folklore* 68 (1955): 224-28.

Smith, Helen Evertson. *Colonial Days and Ways.* New York: Frederick Ungar, 1966.

Snyder, Allegra. "The Dance Symbol." In *New Dimensions in Dance Research: Anthropology and Dance (The American Indian).* New York: Committee on Research in Dance, 1974, pp. 213-24.

Spicer, Edward. "Persistent Cultural Systems." *Science* 174 (1971): 795-800.

Stanard, Mary Newton. *Colonial Virginia: Its People and Customs.* Detroit: Singing Tree Press, 1970.

Stanford, Thomas. *A Linquistic Analysis of Music and Dance Terms from Three Sixteenth-Century Dictionaries of Mexican Indian Languages.* Institute of Latin American Studies Offprint Series No. 76. Austin: The University of Texas Press, 1966.

Stearns, Marshall, and Jean Stearns. *Jazz Dance.* New York: Macmillan, 1968.

Steward, Julian. "A Uintah Ute Bear Dance." *American Anthropologist* 34 (1932): 263-73.

Strauss, Gloria. "The Art of the Sleeve in Chinese Dance." *Dance Perspectives* No. 63, 1975.

Taubert, Gottfried. *Rechtschaffener Tanzmeister.* Leipzig: F. Lanckischens, 1717.

Textor, Robert. *A Cross-Cultural Summary.* New Haven: Human Relations Area Files Press, 1967.

Thompson, Robert Farris. *African Art in Motion.* Berkeley: University of California Press, 1974.

Tomlinson, Kellom. *Six Dances.* London: Tomlinson, 1720.

Turley, Frank. "War Dance Styles." *Powwow Trails* 3 (1966): 18-19.

Tylor, Edward B. *Religion in Primitive Culture.* New York: Harper and Row, 1958.

Vaganova, Agrippina. *Osnovui Klasicheskovo Tantsa.* Moskva: Izdatelstvo "Iskystvo," 1963.

Van Velsen, J. "The Extended-case Method and Situational Analysis." In *The Craft of Social Anthropology.* A.L. Epstein, ed. London: Tavistock, 1967.

Wagner, Roy. *The Invention of Culture.* Englewood Cliffs, N.J.: Prentice-Hall, 1975.

Waterman, Richard. "Role of Dance in Human Society." *Focus on Dance II.* Washington, D.C.: American Association for Health, Physical Education and Recreation.

Williams, Drid. "Review Number Two [Choreometrics]." *CORD News* 6 (1974): 25-29.

References Cited

Wilson, Monica. "The Wedding Cakes: a Study of Ritual Change." In *The Interpretation of Ritual*. J.S. La Fontaine, ed. London: Tavistock, 1972.

Wolfram, Richard. "The Weapon Dances of Europe." *Ethnomusicology* 6 (1962): 186-87.

Young, John Russell, ed. *Memorial History of the City of Philadelphia*. Vol II. New York: New York History Company, 1898.

Žganec, Vinko, ed. *Rad Kongresa Folklorista Jugoslavije Zagreb:* Izdanje i Naklafa Saveza Udruzenja Folklorista Jugoslavije, 1958.

Zorn, Friedrich. *Grammatik der Tanzkunst*. Leipzig: J.J. Weber, 1887.

NOTES

1. Studies that concerned themselves with change also used dance material. Using the Uintah Ute bear dance as an example, Julian Steward talked of the value of studying change by using dance data (1932). Both Steward and Gamble spoke of the increasing secularization in Kiowa Indian dances and related it to other aspects of Kiowa culture involved in the same process (Gamble, 1960).

2. The terms "basic step" and "conventional step" refer to the manner in which a notational scheme divides a movement sequence into minimal notated segments. A notational scheme using basic steps attempts to break the movement sequence down into the shortest customary movements, so that none of these basic steps include shorter basic steps or segmentable parts of other basic steps. The correct description of a movement sequence, then, consists of a simple, determinate sequence of names or symbols denoting distinct, irreducible basic steps. While the development of a set of basic steps might be accomplished by contrastive analysis alone, historically the development of notational schemes featuring basic steps has been characterized by logical considerations drawn from geometry and human anatomy. Notational schemes based on conventional steps do not involve this sort of analysis. Instead, named conventional movement patterns, regardless of length and complexity, are coded directly into the system. The conventional terminologies of classical ballet or American square dance are of this type.

Of interest are certain movement traditions that have basic step terminologies partially supplemented by conventional step terminologies. For example, American West Coast trampoline terminology includes a complete descriptive basic step terminology built up of quarter turn notations of the body in three directions (foreward, back, and twist), body-attitude designations (tuck, pike, layout), time sequence designations, and so on. There are also perhaps a dozen conventional terms to describe certain complex sequences (Brani, Rudolf, Adolf, Swivel-hips). Thus a front somersault with a half twist is also a Brani. As would be expected, those movement sequences of especial importance as units in performance routines are more likely to have conventional names. Likewise, in American tap dancing a pedagogical de-

228

scriptive system (actually several) using basic steps (jump-shuffle-shuffle-step-step, etc.) coexists with conventional terms such as "falling-off-a-log," denoting complex performance units.

Finally, the distinction between basic step and conventional step refers to the analytical pretensions of the notational schemes and not to the actual "complexity," or whatever, of the steps themselves. It is conceivable that one author's notational scheme based on conventional steps might, in fact, approximate another's attempt to produce one based on basic steps. And it will readily be appreciated that the basic steps of an author writing in another tradition in an earlier age, say those of Feuillet, for example, may not appear very basic after all. What is significant here is what the analyst was attempting to do when he did it (R. Royce, personal communication).

3. A fourth movement notation system deserves mention although it does not yet enjoy the widespread use of the three others discussed in the text. I refer to that system developed between 1951 and 1956 by Noa Eshkol and Abraham Wachmann and known as Eshkol-Wachmann movement notation. Developed initially in Israel for the purpose of notating folk dance, it has since been applied to a variety of subjects including classical ballet, physical education, sign language of the deaf, the Feldenkrais physiotherapeutical method, and movement behavior of golden jackals, Tasmanian devils, and wolf pups. In Eshkol-Wachmann, discrete and continuous aspects of movement are described by notating each movement in terms of its initial position, its final position, and the trajectory between the two positions. Notated movements are of three kinds: rotatory, conical, and plane. The notation is based on a coordinate system of reference with horizontal and vertical components projected onto the surface of a sphere. One important concept of Eshkol-Wachmann notation is the "Law of Light and Heavy Limbs." Light limbs, carried by the heavy limbs, can change their position in space as a result of the movement of the heavy limbs. Initially used only in Israel, the Eshkol-Wachmann notation system has expanded both geographically and in terms of the variety of movement it has shown it can record (Deborah A. Champagne, personal communication).

4. Bartenieff comments that current work in teaching and notating involves experimenting with combining the strengths of Labanotation and Effort-Shape in a truly complementary way (personal communication).

5. The case study focuses on social dance in the middle colonies of Pennsylvania, New York, and Virginia during the eighteenth century.

6. The observations on which this study is based were carried out during 1970. I was then a graduate student in the department of anthropology at the University of California Berkeley campus and was supported by a training grant from the National Institutes of Health. I am grateful to NIH for its financial support, to George M. Foster, the administrator of the grant, and to the participants and spectators of the Oakland and San Francisco powwows,

who were gracious and understanding of my presence. Some of this case study material was presented as a paper at the annual meeting of the American Folklore Society in November of 1970.

7. See Ablon, "Relocated Indians in the San Francisco Bay Area: Social Interaction and Indian Identity," *Human Organization* 23:1964, 296-304.

8. "Drum" is used to mean a group of men who both drum and sing.

9. Judith Lynne Hanna and Drid Williams are two of the few doing systematic research in the area of the semantics of dance.

INDEX

231

Index

232

Index

Index

234

Index

Index

Index

Index